POWER WRITING

POWER WRITING

20 Powerful Principles for Clear and Effective Writing

BRANDON ROYAL

JAICO PUBLISHING HOUSE

Ahmedabad Bangalore Chennai
Delhi Hyderabad Kolkata Mumbai

Published by Jaico Publishing House
A-2 Jash Chambers, 7-A Sir Phirozshah Mehta Road
Fort, Mumbai - 400 001
jaicopub@jaicobooks.com
www.jaicobooks.com

© Brandon Royal

Published in arrangement with
Maven Publishing
4520 Manilla Road S.E.
Calgary, Alberta, Canada T2G 4B7

To be sold only in India, Bangladesh, Bhutan,
Pakistan, Nepal, Sri Lanka and the Maldives.

POWER WRITING
ISBN 978-81-8495-727-3

First Jaico Impression: 2015
Fourth Jaico Impression: 2017

No part of this book may be reproduced or utilized in
any form or by any means, electronic or
mechanical including photocopying, recording or by any
information storage and retrieval system,
without permission in writing from the publishers.

Printed by
Trinity Academy For Corporate Training Limited, Mumbai

Contents

Part III: Readability

Dedication

This book is dedicated to anyone with an interest in writing, but especially to writing teachers and writing students. The reciprocal nature of teaching requires that the teacher must always remain a student, and that the student, through his or her questions and struggles, ultimately drives the learning process.

Introduction

This book is based on a simple but powerful observation: Students and young professionals who develop outstanding writing skills do so primarily by mastering a limited number of the most important writing principles, which they use over and over again. What are these recurring principles? The answer to this question is the basis of this material. Within these pages are twenty immutable principles of writing.

Writing has four pillars—structure, style, readability, and grammar—and each pillar is like the single leg of a sturdy chair. Structure is about organization and deciding in which order to present your ideas. Style describes how one writes, including how to use specific examples to support what is written. Readability is about presentation and how to make a document visually pleasing and easy to read. Grammar, including diction, is about expressing language in a correct and acceptable form. This book addresses the first three pillars; the fourth pillar, grammar, is given extensive coverage in *Power Grammar*. Because of the pervasive nature of writing, this guidebook is suitable for a wide-ranging audience, including writing aficionados from all walks of life. High school and college students can use this material for supplementary study. Businesspersons can use this material as a refresher course. Individuals preparing for job placement tests and students preparing for college or graduate entrance exams will benefit from a time-tested review of basic writing principles and rules.

Let's get started.

Part I

Structure

I'm sorry to have written such a long letter. If I had had more time, I could have written a shorter one.

—Blaise Pascal

Principle 1

Write With a Top-Down Approach

☞ Principle #1: Write your conclusion and place it first.

Writing done for everyday purposes falls into the category of expository writing, which includes newspaper articles, college essays, and business memos and letters. Expository writing explains and often summarizes a topic or issue. Strategically, the summary or conclusion should come at the beginning of an expository piece, not at the end. The reader is first told what the writing is about, then given the supporting facts or details. This way, the reader is not left guessing at the writer's main idea.

Whereas the primary purpose of expository writing is to explain, inform, or persuade, the primary purpose of fiction or creative writing is to enlighten or entertain. As far as fiction and creative writing are concerned, it is fine (even desirable) to delay the conclusion, as in the case of a surprise ending. But the hard-and-fast rule in expository writing is that we should not keep our conclusion from the reader. We should come out with it right away. When our purpose is to explain or inform, don't play, "I've got a secret."

Experienced writing instructors know that one of the easiest ways to fix students' writing is to have them place their conclusions near the top of the page, not the bottom. Instructors are fond of a trick that involves asking students to write a short piece on a random topic and, upon completion, walking up to each student without reading what he or she has written, circling the last sentence, and moving it to the very top of the page. In a majority of cases, instructors know that the last lines written contain the conclusion. This technique is known as BLOT, or "bottom line on top." It is human nature, and it seems logical, that we should conclude at the end rather than the beginning. But writing should be top-down, structured in the inverted pyramid style. The broad base of the inverted pyramid is analogous to the broad conclusion set forth at the beginning of a piece.

Favor the top-down approach to writing:

Most Important☺

Next Most Important

Next Most Important

Least Important

Avoid the bottom-up approach to writing:

Least Important

Next Most Important

Next Most Important

Most Important☹

The newspaper industry depends upon the top-down technique of writing. Reporters know that if their stories cannot fit into the allocated space, their editors will cut from the bottom up. Therefore, conclusions generally cannot appear in the last lines, which are reserved for minor details.

Errors of writing often mimic errors in conversation. When we write, we should think about giving the reader a destination first before giving him or her the directions on how to get there. If we fail to do this, we will not get our message across in the most effective way. The value of a top-down approach in real life conversation occurs in the following dialogue.

POOR VERSION

Dialogue between two coworkers:

"Alice, can you do something for me when you're downtown? If you're taking the subway to Main Street, get off and take the first exit out of the subway and walk down to Cross Street. At the intersection of Cross Street and Vine, you'll find Sandy's Stationery Store. Can you go in and pick up a pack of Pentel 0.5mm lead refills?"

BETTER VERSION

Dialogue between two coworkers:

Alice, can you do something for me when you're downtown? I need a pack of Pentel 0.5mm lead refills. The best place to get them is Sandy's Stationery Store. You can take the subway to Main Street, get off and take the first exit out of the subway and walk down to Cross Street. The store is at the intersection of Cross Street and Vine.

The conclusion is underlined in each version. Note how annoying the first version can be from the listener's perspective. If you have encountered a similar situation in everyday life, you may have felt like screaming. Once you finally find out what the speaker's point is, you might have to ask him or her to repeat everything so you can remember the details. The same holds true for writing. It is just as frustrating when you are reading a piece of writing and you do not know where the discussion is going.

Conceptually, we want to think in terms of a descending writing structure—one in which we move "downhill" from conclusion to details rather than "uphill" from details to conclusion.

Compare the following two versions of the same piece of business writing. In evaluating the two samples, we find that the second one is more top-down in its approach. The conclusion is at the top: "Asia and Africa represent the biggest future international market for basic consumer goods if population is used as a measure." Also, the second version uses statistics solely as detail.

LESS EFFECTIVE

Three-fourths of the world's people currently live in Asia and Africa—from South Africa to the Sahara, from the Middle East to Japan, from Siberia to Indonesia. This population statistic is quite revealing. If we selectively and representatively choose four persons from the entire world, here is what the probable outcome would be. One person would be from China, one would be from India, and one more would be from somewhere else in Asia or Africa. The fourth person would have to be chosen from all of North America, South America, Europe, and Oceania!

Basic consumer goods represent durable and nondurable daily necessities, including food and cooking utensils, clothing and textiles, toiletries, electronics, home furnishings, and mechanized and miscellaneous household products. Hence, Asia and Africa represent the biggest future international market for basic consumer goods if population is used as a measure.

MORE EFFECTIVE

Asia and Africa represent the biggest future international market for basic consumer goods if population is used as a measure. Basic consumer goods represent durable and nondurable daily necessities, including food and cooking utensils, clothing and textiles, toiletries, electronics, home furnishings, and mechanized and miscellaneous household products.

Three-fourths of the world's people currently live in Asia and Africa—from South Africa to the Sahara, from the Middle East to Japan, from Siberia to Indonesia. This population statistic is quite revealing. If we selectively and representatively choose four persons from the entire world, here is what the probable outcome would be. One person would be from China, one would be from India, and one more would be from somewhere else in Asia or Africa. The fourth person would have to be chosen from all of North America, South America, Europe, and Oceania!

Now review this piece:

Hundreds of people packed into the auditorium seats on the evening of December 29. Being one of twelve opening performers, I was granted the opportunity to dance on stage for the first time in my life. Although my part only lasted five minutes, those five minutes became a significant moment in my life. Ever since rehearsals began two months before, I had spent many hours practicing on my own, in addition to the normal rehearsal sessions. Whether on a bus, waiting in a doctor's office, or walking to work, I always had my MP3 player on, listening to the music and trying to go through the steps in my mind over and over again. I was determined to do my best. Despite my best preparation, my nervousness caused me to slip during the performance. All of a sudden, my mind turned blank. I stood there, not knowing how to react to the music. Fifteen seconds seemed like 15 hours in a normal day.

The conclusion as underlined above is either well placed or ill placed depending on the writer's purpose in writing the passage. If the purpose is to inform the reader, then it is ill placed because the conclusion should be placed nearer the top. But as this is likely a creative writing piece, meant to entertain, the conclusion can be delayed. Just remember the rule of expository writing that governs everyday writing: Your conclusion should be at or very near the beginning of your written piece.

> An airline pilot never leaves the runway without having a destination and flight pattern. When our purpose in writing is to explain or inform, we should conclude first then concentrate on supporting details. Don't play "I've got a secret."

Principle 2

Break Things Down

☞ Principle #2: **Break your subject into two to four major parts and use a lead sentence.**

Assuming that you know what you want to write about, you must decide what basic building blocks will comprise your work. You can break your subject into two to four major parts. Three parts are typically recommended, but for the sake of simplicity, no more than four categories should be introduced. The classic "five-paragraph" approach to writing can be used to outline, in one paragraph, any writing piece. In the example on page 21, all you have to do is supply the colors!

LEAD SENTENCES VS. TOPIC SENTENCES

Once you have broken down your topic into two to four major categories, next you will want to elaborate on these ideas. Consider using a *lead sentence,* which is similar to a *topic sentence.* Whereas a topic sentence summarizes the contents of a single paragraph within an essay or report, a lead sentence summarizes the contents of an entire essay or report. Placed at the beginning of a piece, it foreshadows what is to come, highlighting what items will be discussed and, typically, the order in which they will be discussed. Each item in the lead should be developed into at least one separate paragraph within the body of the essay or report. For example, in a personal essay, this sentence could serve as an introduction or lead:

I would like to show who I am through a discussion of three special turning points in my personal and career development: when I went to university on a lacrosse scholarship, when I spent a year with the Peace Corps, and when I joined a commodity trading firm in London.

In a business report, the following could serve as a lead sentence, placed at the beginning of a report:

Based on information taken from a recent survey, this report summarizes the three biggest problems that our company faces: namely, employee turnover, store thefts, and poor customer service.

> The number three is a magic number in writing. Think of building your writing around three key ideas or concepts.

FINDING TWO TO FOUR MAJOR IDEAS

Introduction

Colors make the world bright and full. My favorite colors are green, blue, and yellow. Each of these colors is special to me. ____ ____ ________________________.

Body

Green is like the green grass that blankets the earth______ ____ ____ ____.

Blue is like the sky that soars high above. ______________ ____ ____ __________.

Yellow is like the sun that shines so brightly. ___________ ____ ____ ___________________.

Conclusion

Green is the most interesting of all these colors. Even the colors blue and yellow combine to form green. _______ ____ ____ ________.

OUTLINES FOR BUSINESS REPORT WRITING

The following page contains sample outlines for the four classic types of business reports. Although it is useful to think of all expository writing as having an introduction, body, and conclusion, in the case of business reports, the word "findings" is typically substituted for the word "body." Note though that the "findings" section, as shown on the next page, is broken down into three to four categories. Business reports include executive summaries (usually one page) and recommendations (usually two pages). An executive summary is "a summary of the writer's findings, conclusions, and recommendations." It comes first in the report but is written last. A recommendation is "a statement of what the writer thinks should be done as a result of his or her conclusions."

Business reports can serve one of four purposes: (1) feasibility study, (2) comparative study, (3) evaluation study, and (4) cost study. One way to summarize the differences among these reports is to take a hypothetical example from the world of business. Let's choose the Wonderland Hotel chain, which is considering expanding its operations to Jakarta, Indonesia. First, a *feasibility study report* is required. Executives at the head office must ask, "Is the hotel market in Jakarta sufficiently large enough to ensure that our hotel can prosper?" Next, assuming the hotel is built and operational, executives at regional headquarters may ask: "How do operations, including revenues, expenses, and profits, compare between the Singapore Wonderland Hotel and the Jakarta Wonderland Hotel?" This question forms the basis of a *comparative study report*. Next, the manager of the Jakarta Wonderland Hotel, who wants to increase hotel service to its customers, issues a questionnaire for guests to fill out. The questionnaire, titled "Are You Satisfied?," forms the basis of an *evaluation study report*. Finally, the manager of the Jakarta Wonderland Hotel, based on results from its survey, seeks authorization to build a water slide, games room, and reading room—all things that guests say they want. How much will it cost to build a water slide, games room and reading room? This question forms the basis of a *cost study report*.

Feasibility Study Report Comparative Study Report

Executive Summary

Contents

Introduction

Findings

2.1 Size of the market
2.2 Competitors
2.3 Market entry strategy
2.4 Financing of operations

Conclusions

Recommendations

Appendixes

Executive Summary

Contents

Introduction

Findings

2.1 Revenue analysis
2.2 Expense analysis
2.3 Profit analysis

Conclusions

Recommendations

Appendixes

Evaluation Study Report Cost Study Report

Executive Summary

Contents

Introduction

Findings

2.1 Questionnaire
2.2 Evaluation of customer ratings from 1 to 5
2.3 Evaluation of written responses

Conclusions

Recommendations

Appendixes

Executive Summary

Contents

Introduction

Findings

2.1 Water slide
2.2 Games room
2.3 Reading room

Conclusions

Recommendations

Appendixes

Principle 3

Use Transition Words

☞ Principle #3: Use transition words to signal the flow of your writing.

"Transition" words, such as *but* and *however,* have been called the traffic lights of language. They serve one of four primary purposes: to show contrast, illustration, continuation, or conclusion. On the next page, you will see transition words highlighted in two sample paragraphs. Words of illustration include *first, second, for instance,* and *for example. So* signals conclusion. *However* signals contrast. *Moreover* signals continuation.

Transition words appear underlined in the following examples.

EXAMPLE 1

Time management involves thinking in terms of effectiveness first and efficiency second. Whereas efficiency is concerned with doing a task in the fastest possible manner, effectiveness is concerned with spending time doing the "right" things. Effectiveness is therefore a broader, more useful concept, which questions whether we should even do a particular task.

EXAMPLE 2

The process of evolution takes two distinct forms: organic and exosomatic. In the first, which is commonly called Darwinian evolution, a plant or animal develops a genetic mutation that may be either helpful or harmful. If the change is helpful, the organism is favored by the process of natural selection and flourishes; if it is harmful, the organism suffers and eventually dies out.

The whole of what we call human culture, on the other hand, is a result of exosomatic evolution. Such a change may be gradual, but it represents conscious choices that enable human beings to adapt to environments that would otherwise be inimical to their survival.

EXAMPLE 3

How does the world's deadliest snake differ from the world's most dangerous snake? The world's deadliest snake is the one that is the most venomous while the world's most dangerous snake is the one that kills the most people. Undoubtably, the Belcher Sea Snake is the world's deadliest; a few milligrams of its venom can kill 1,000 people. This docile snake, however, rarely comes into contact with humans.

The Carpet Viper kills the most people each year so it is considered the world's most dangerous snake. Some 20,000 people living throughout Africa and Asia lose their lives to this snake species each year.

Coincidentally, what is the world's most feared snake? This "title" is likely held by the Black Mamba. Africa's longest and fastest snake, this highly venomous, ill-tempered, and unpredictable snake is known to attack even when not provoked.

THE FOUR TYPES OF TRANSITION WORDS

I. Continuation Words

GREEN LIGHT
"Keep going in the same direction"

Examples:
•moreover •furthermore
•on the one hand
•undoubtedly
•coincidentally

II. Illustration Words

FLASHING GREEN
"Slow down and be watchful"

Examples:
•first, second, third
•for example •for instance •in fact
•case in point

III. Contrast Words

FLASHING YELLOW
"Get ready to turn"

Examples:
•however
•but •yet
•on the other hand
•whereas •while
•conversely

IV. Conclusion Words

RED LIGHT
"You're about to arrive"

Examples:
•in conclusion
•finally •clearly
•hence •so •thus
•therefore
•as a result

Exercise

Read the sentences below, arranging them in a manner that makes the most sense in terms of logic and flow. You'll find the suggested solutions on page 119.

TOPIC: THE WHALE

1. When people think of ants, on the other hand, they tend to think of hardworking, underfed creatures, transporting objects twice their body size to and from hidden hideaways.

2. When most people think of whales, they think of sluggish, obese animals, frolicking freely in the ocean and eating tons of food to sustain themselves.

3. In fact, when we compare the proportionate food consumption of all living creatures, we find that the whale is one of the most food-efficient creatures on earth.

4. However, if we analyze food consumption based on body size, we find that ants eat their full body weight every day, while a whale eats the equivalent of only one-thousandth of its body weight each day.

5. The whale is the largest mammal in the animal kingdom.

THE SIMPLEST WRITING APPROACH

Here is a sure-fire way to write just about anything. It might not be the most exciting writing structure, but it is clear and it works.

Instructions

1. Take a stance.
2. Write your conclusion.
3. State "There are several reasons for this."
4. Use transition words. Voilà.

EXAMPLE TOPIC: RENAISSANCE

The Renaissance period was the most glorious time in human history. There are several reasons for this. First, ____

____

____

__________ Second, ______________________________

____

______________________________________ Third, ____________

____

____________________ For instance, ____________________

____

______________________________ Moreover ______________

____

____

______________________________ Finally, ______________

____

____________________________.

Principle 4

Review the Six Basic Writing Structures

☞ Principle #4: **Use the six basic writing structures to put ideas in their proper order.**

Writing is very much about the order of ideas presented and the emphasis given to them. In terms of order, we expect ideas to unfold logically, which typically means seeing the most important ideas first. In terms of emphasis, we expect the most important ideas to get the most coverage. The six commonly used structures in writing include: (1) categorical, (2) evaluative, (3) chronological, (4) comparative, (5) sequential, and (6) causal.

The emphasis or weight given to ideas is important in all structures. The more you write about something, the more important that idea or topic is deemed to be. Order is also important, but not of paramount importance in all cases. Structures in which order is important include chronological, comparative, sequential, and causal structures. In chronological structures, you discuss the earliest events first and move forward in time. In comparative structures, the most important ideas come before any others. In sequential structures, you begin with the first item in a sequence and end with the last item in the sequence. In cause-and-effect structures, causes are usually identified and discussed before their effects.

In other structures, order is less important. These include categorical and evaluative structures. If we choose to structure our writing by category, it will not make much difference whether we talk about America, China, and then Britain, or start with Britain, go on to China, and finish with America. The same is true with structures based on evaluation; it generally makes little difference whether we discuss pros first and cons second or cons first and pros last. Moreover, if the writer wants to emphasize one side more than the other (or one idea more than another), he or she should make sure the conclusion does this.

Although not considered classic writing structures, two other common writing formats include "Question and Answer" and "Problem and Solution." These structures tend to be less formal, and are often used with memos, handouts, and flyers.

NOTE ✍ Writing structures relate to the body of a writing piece, not to the introduction or conclusion.

> Zoology 101: You can tell what kind of animal it is by looking at the skeleton. Structure informs content. Important ideas in writing demand the most attention and get discussed first.

SUMMARY OF THE SIX WRITING STRUCTURES

	Structure	Proper Order	Examples
1	**Categorical** • Item 1, item 2, item 3 • A, B or B, A • A, B, C or C, B, A	• Discuss items in any order.	**2 items** • Let's talk about apples and oranges. **3 items** • Let's talk about America, China, and Britain.
2	**Evaluative** • Pros and cons • Positives and negatives • Pluses and minuses	• Discuss the pro-side first, then the con-side (or vice versa).	**2 items** • Let's talk about the weather: sunny but humid. **3 items** • Let's talk about what voters think: those for, those against, and those undecided.
3	**Chronological** • Past, present, future • Before, during, after	• Discuss early events first, followed by later events.	**2 items** • Let's talk about sales from January to June. **3 items** • Let's talk about Europe's economy: 1800s, 1900s, and the year 2000 and beyond.

	Structure	Proper Order	Examples
4	**Comparative** • A > B; B > A • C > B > A • C > A or B	• Discuss most relevant contrasting features first; discuss less important features next.	**2 items** • Let's discuss our most important goals and our minor goals. **3 items** • Let's compare our company to our competitors' size, products, and people/resources.
5	**Sequential** • 1st, 2nd, 3rd • X to Y to Z (or reverse)	• Discuss items in order of sequence, from first to last (or in reverse).	**2 items** • Let's discuss drug addiction that progresses from soft drugs to hard drugs. **3 items** • Let's talk about lawmaking at the municipal, state, and national levels.
6	**Causal** • A leads to B • A and B lead to C • $A \rightarrow B$ • $A + B \rightarrow C$	• Discuss early events first, followed by later events (or vice versa).	**2 items** • Let's talk about whether the increase in unemployment is the cause of the increase in crime. **3 items** • Let's talk about the primary causes of global warming, the likely effects of global warming, and the controversy surrounding the issue.

OUTLINES FOR THE SIX WRITING STRUCTURES

The following are sample outlines highlighting the six types of writing structures.

CATEGORICAL

Introduction

Let's discuss three countries.

America ...

China ...

Britain ...

Conclusion

COMPARATIVE

Introduction

Let's compare our company to our competitors.

In terms of size ...

In terms of products and services ...

In terms of people and resources ...

Conclusion

EVALUATIVE

Introduction

Let's evaluate what voters think.

Those for our party ...

Those against our party ...

Those still undecided ...

Conclusion

SEQUENTIAL

Introduction

Let's discuss lawmaking hierarchy at three levels.

At the municipal level ...

At the state level ...

At the national level ...

Conclusion

CHRONOLOGICAL

Introduction

Let's discuss the economy of Europe.

In the 1800s ...

In the 1900s ...

In the year 2000 and beyond ...

Conclusion

CAUSAL

Introduction

Let's discuss the primary causes and likely effects of global warming.

The primary causes are ...

The likely effects are ...

The controversy is ...

Conclusion

Below are two representative samples of "Question and Answer" and "Problem and Solution" formats. One you might find as part of a travel brochure; the other you might find as part of a business memo.

QUESTION AND ANSWER EXAMPLE

Question: *What is the best way to visit another country?*

Answer: *Take only pictures and leave only footprints.*

Question: *How can we help protect endangered animals?*

Answer: *Fight against loss of animal habitat, prosecute poachers, and prohibit the sale or purchase of endangered animals and their by-products.*

PROBLEM AND SOLUTION EXAMPLE

During our annual conference, many corporate issues were raised. Here is a list of problems cited and our proposed solutions.

Problem: *High employee turnover.*

Solution: *Put more effort into recruiting; establish an in-house training program; institute weekly happy hours each Friday, paid for by the company.*

Problem: *Increased marketplace competition.*

Solution: *Redefine our company focus; discontinue products and product lines that fail the 80-20 rule; hold employee brainstorming sessions in hopes of finding new ideas and creative solutions.*

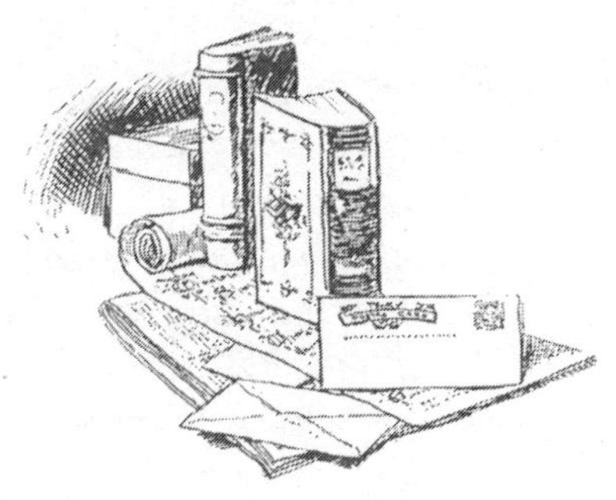

Principle 5

Keep Like Things Together

☞ Principle #5: **Finish discussing one topic before going on to discuss other topics.**

Imagine visiting the zoo to find that all the animals were in one big cage. It would not only be dangerous for the animals but also nearly impossible for visitors to view the animals in a coherent manner. Unfortunately, sometimes a piece of writing can be like a zoo, in which all of the different animals (ideas) are in one big cage, running wild. When we write (as when we speak), the ideas we describe should be grouped together. It is best to finish discussing one idea before going on to discuss another.

Here's an example of an essay with jumbled ideas.

ORIGINAL VERSION

In 1981, Roger Sperry received the Nobel Prize for his proof of the split-brain theory. According to Dr. Sperry, the brain has two hemispheres with different, but overlapping functions.

The left side of the brain is responsible for analytical, linear, verbal, and rational thought. Left-brain thinking is "spotlight" thinking. The right hemisphere is holistic, imaginative, nonverbal, and artistic. It is the left brain that a person relies on when balancing a checkbook, remembering names and dates, or setting goals and objectives. Whenever a person recalls another person's face, becomes engrossed in a symphony, or simply daydreams, that person is engaging in right-brain functions. Right-brain thinking is "floodlight" thinking and right-brain processes are, to the chagrin of many, less often rewarded in school. Since most of the Western concepts of thinking come from Greek logic, which is a linear logic system, left-brained processes are most rewarded in the western educational system.

In summary, the right and left hemispheres of the brain each specialize in distinct types of thinking processes. In the most basic sense, the left brain is the analytical side while the right brain is the creative side.

Note that although the above writing piece employs a classic structure—containing an introduction, body, and conclusion—the content is difficult to read and absorb because ideas are tangled. If this discussion were to continue for a couple of pages, the reader might feel that his or her mind had turned to spaghetti. We know that there are two things under discussion—left-brain versus right-brain thinking—but the technique with which ideas are described and supported is deficient.

CORRECTED VERSION 1

In 1981, Roger Sperry received the Nobel Prize for his proof of the split-brain theory. According to Dr. Perry, the brain has two hemispheres with different but overlapping functions. Each hemisphere of the brain specializes in distinct types of thinking processes. In the most basic sense, the left brain is the analytical side while the right brain is the creative side.

The left side of the brain is responsible for analytical, linear, verbal, and rational thought. Left-brain thinking is characterized as "spotlight" thinking. It is the left brain that a person relies on when balancing a checkbook, remembering names and dates, or setting goals and objectives. The right hemisphere is holistic, imaginative, nonverbal, and artistic. Right-brain thinking is characterized as "floodlight" thinking. Whenever a person recalls another person's face, becomes engrossed in a symphony, or simply daydreams, that person is engaged in right-brain functions.

Since most Western concepts of thinking are derived from Greek logic, which is a linear logic system, left-brained processes are most rewarded in the Western education system. Right-brain processes are, to the chagrin of many, less often rewarded in school.

In the corrected example above, we also have classic usage of introduction, body, and conclusion. The structure in the second paragraph proceeds as follows: left-brain thinking is described within the first two sentences, followed by a third supporting sentence which includes examples of left-brain thinking. Right-brain thinking is then described in two sentences, followed by a supporting sentence which includes examples of right-brain thinking. The third paragraph concludes with an implication of left- and right-brain thinking.

CORRECTED VERSION 2

In 1981, Roger Sperry received the Nobel Prize for his proof of the split-brain theory. According to Dr. Perry, the brain has two hemispheres with different but overlapping functions. Each hemisphere of the brain specializes in distinct types of thinking processes. In the most basic sense, the left brain is the analytical side while the right brain is the creative side.

The left side of the brain is responsible for analytical, linear, verbal, and rational thought. Left-brain thinking is characterized as "spotlight" thinking. It is the left brain that a person relies on when balancing a checkbook, remembering names and dates, or setting goals and objectives. Since most Western concepts of thinking are derived from Greek logic, which is a linear logic system, left-brained processes are most rewarded in the Western education system.

The right hemisphere is holistic, imaginative, nonverbal, and artistic. Right-brain thinking is characterized as "floodlight" thinking. Whenever a person recalls another person's face, becomes engrossed in a symphony, or simply daydreams, that person is engaged in right-brain functions. Right-brain processes are, to the chagrin of many, less often rewarded in school.

The three-paragraph structure above is also a classic one: an introduction is followed by two paragraphs, each dedicated entirely to either left- or right-brain thinking. In the second paragraph, left-brain thinking is described within the first two sentences, followed by a third supporting sentence containing examples of this type of thinking, and a concluding sentence highlighting an implication of left-brain thinking. In the third paragraph, right-brain thinking is described in two sentences, followed by a supporting sentence with examples of this type of thinking, and finally a one sentence implication of right-brain thinking.

Part II
Style

When Calvin Coolidge was asked by his wife what the preacher had preached on, he replied "Sin," and, when asked what the preacher had said, replied "He was against it." Mr. Coolidge was brief but one hardly envies Mrs. Coolidge.

—F.L. Lucas

Principle 6

Support What You Say

☞ Principle #6: **Use specific and concrete words to support what you say.**

One major difference between good writing and mediocre writing lies with the specific and concrete examples that you use or fail to use. Say, for example, you are writing about an apple. Not all apples are identical. What kind of apple is it? Golden Delicious, Gala, Fuji, McIntosh, Granny Smith? What color is it? What shape is it? How does it taste? What is its texture? Where is it grown? Let's look at an example in a business context. Suppose you hear that your company's profits are down. What are the specifics? Did the sales volume decline? Was the sales price reduced? Did costs go up? And, if any of the above, then by how much?

Note the difference in each of the following statements:

GENERAL

Corporate profits decreased.

BETTER BUT STILL NOT SPECIFIC

Corporate profits decreased because costs increased.

SPECIFIC

Corporate profits decreased by 10 percent as overall costs increased by 20 percent.

EVEN BETTER

Corporate profits decreased by 10 percent as overall costs increased by 20 percent. In particular, higher salary expenses were the major reason for the increase in costs. Higher salary costs were primarily the result of increases in executive compensation; the aggregate wages paid to factory workers actually decreased by 5 percent due to a decrease in the number of overtime hours clocked.

Examples and details are the very things people remember long after reading a piece. Compare the two examples below describing the popular attitude toward science.

VERSION 1

The popular attitude toward science in the United States is a mix of superstition and awe. Quaint folklore portrays scientific genius as solitary and requiring no nurture. Within the public imagination, such pleasant thoughts go undisturbed by the reality of today's large research labs.

VERSION 2

The popular attitude toward science in the United States is a mix of superstition and awe. Quaint folklore portrays scientific genius as solitary and requiring no nurture. Within the public imagination are visions of the Wright Brothers at work in their bicycle shop, contriving the first flying machine, and of Thomas Edison plumbing the mysteries of electricity with a few magnets and some pieces of wire. Such pleasant thoughts go undisturbed by today's large research labs, whose members undergo highly specialized training in order to work on narrowly defined research problems.

The second version uses examples drawn from the Wright Brothers and Thomas Edison. This helps us visualize what the author is saying.

Consider the two memos below. Which one would convince you to attend the Calgary Stampede and Exhibition?

MEMO 1

The Calgary Stampede will be held during the first week of July. There will be loads of activities, fun, and food for all. Bring your cowboy hat and boots. See you there!

MEMO 2

The Calgary Stampede will be held during the first week of July. The exhibition grounds are home to two dozen midway rides, a myriad of food stalls (try those miniature doughnuts!), the sounds of live country music, First Nations exhibits, bustling saloons, and a large casino. For the youngsters, there is a petting zoo, magic tricks, and loads of games, with the chance to win giant stuffed animals. The opening day parade has a flotilla of floats, and daily rodeo events including calf roping, bull riding, and chuck wagon races. Fantastic fireworks each evening. See you there!

Note that the second and better example is longer than the original. Given that writing should be concise, why is the shorter example not better? A trade-off exists between brevity and detail. Sufficient detail will make a piece of writing longer, but this does not necessarily indicate wordiness. Conciseness requires a minimum number of words at the sentence level, whereas sufficient support may require more sentences.

Here is a more humorous example. Consider which of the following better demonstrates to you that a physical book is a wonderful tool.

BLURB 1

Books are marvelous tools. They're informative and entertaining, and they are here to stay.

BLURB 2

The book is a revolutionary breakthrough in modern technology. No wires, no circuits, no batteries. Nothing to be connected or switched on. It's so easy, even a child can operate it. Just lift its cover! Compact and portable, it can be used anywhere—even sitting in an armchair by the fire. Yet it is powerful enough to hold as much information as a CD.

This is how it works: The book may be picked up at any time and used by merely opening it. The book never crashes and never needs rebooting. The browse feature allows you to move instantly to any sheet, and move forward or backward as you wish. Many come with an index feature, which pinpoints the exact location of selected information for instant retrieval. You can also make personal notes next to book entries with an optional programming tool, the Portable Erasable Nib Cryptic Intercommunication Language Stylus (PENCILS).

Is this the end of the computer? The BOOK (Built in Orderly Organized Knowledge) looks as though it will become the entertainment wave of the future.

Vague language weakens your writing because it forces the reader to guess at what you mean instead of allowing him or her to concentrate fully on your ideas and style. Choose specific, descriptive words for more forceful writing. Sometimes, to be specific and concrete, you will have to use more words than usual. That's okay. While it is important to cut unnecessary words, it is even more important to properly support what you say.

Exercise

Rewrite the following sentences to replace vague language with specific, concrete language. Suggested answers are found on pages 119–120.

1. Joannie has a dog and a cat.
2. The vacation was expensive.
3. Rainbows are colorful.
4. Sheila is tall and good-looking.
5. Many economists think that the Federal Reserve Bank is to blame for the current economic downturn.
6. Firms should advertise because advertising will surely increase sales.
7. Tim is a careless person.
8. The contestant was eliminated in the first round because she missed an easy geography question.
9. The store is packed with goods.
10. Mr. and Mrs. Jones make a cute couple.

TRAIN YOURSELF TO CITE SPECIFIC EXAMPLES

Most writing suffers from superficiality—it is too general. Examples abound in both the academic and professional realm. For example, when writing job search letters or college application essays, candidates often write sentences such as: "I have good people skills," "I have strong communication skills," or "I have good analytical skills."

There is a debater's adage: "A statement without support merits a denial without reason." If one person says, "Purple polka-dot bikinis are awful" but gives no evidence to support the statement, another person is entitled to say, "You're wrong," and not give a reason. A valued technique, which can be used when writing rough drafts, is to stress the points you wish to make by placing "for example" immediately after what you write. This will ensure that you lend support to your statements.

NOTE ✍ As a practical matter, each writer should decide whether to leave "for example" in an essay or to edit it out, particularly if looking for a more seamless connection between ideas and support points.

The following sample sentences were taken directly from the essays of applicants applying to college or graduate school.

EXAMPLE 1

Candidate's statement:

I am an energetic, loyal, creative, diligent, honest, strict, humorous, responsible, flexible, and ambitious person.

Reviewer's likely comment:

Would you care to develop your discussion and support a few of these traits with concrete examples?

A real amateur's mistake is to use a "shopping list of traits." This could occur when you are writing to describe yourself (as is the case if writing a personal essay) or when you are writing to describe someone else (as might be the case when writing academic or professional letters of recommendation or job reference letters). Giving adequate support for a dozen traits is practically impossible. The better approach is to choose two or three traits and develop each in more detail.

EXAMPLE 2

Candidate's statement:

Growing up in both the East and West, I have experienced both Asian and Western points of view.

Reviewer's likely comment:

What are these Asian and Western points of view?

EXAMPLE 3

Candidate's statement:

Although ABC Company did not flourish, I still consider my effort a success because I was able to identify strengths and weaknesses in my overall business skills.

Reviewer's likely comment:

What strengths and weaknesses did you identify?

EXAMPLE 4

Candidate's statement:

Not only did I develop important operational skills in running a business but I experienced and witnessed the challenges that entrepreneurs face on a daily basis.

Reviewer's likely comment:

What were these challenges?

The following examples show how unsupported statements can be improved with the addition of concrete details.

ORIGINAL

I was brought up out of context—an English girl in a British colony. I went through 13 years of international school and my primary school had twenty-eight nationalities.

BETTER

I was brought up out of context—an English girl in a British colony. I went through 13 years of international school and my primary school had twenty-eight nationalities. I remember when my fourth-year teacher decided to hold an International Day. Everyone wore a traditional or national costume and brought a dish of traditional cuisine. There is no real national costume for England, so I dressed as an English Rose, and brought Yorkshire Parkin, a sweet ginger cake, as my dish.

ORIGINAL

I grew up in a Maine farm family that was ethnically Scottish, but really your everyday New England household. I am thankful now for a stable, happy childhood. My parents gave me the best education and upbringing they could. They taught me to be caring and respectful of people and the environment. They taught me honesty, humility, and the silliness of pretense.

BETTER

I grew up in a Maine farm family that was ethnically Scottish, but really your everyday New England household. I am thankful now for a stable, happy childhood. My parents gave me the best education and upbringing they could. They took me to museums, libraries, and ballet lessons. They taught me to be caring and respectful of people and the environment. Often they taught by example: When I was four or five, my elder brothers and I accidentally lit a field on fire. Wind caught the flames, and the fire quickly engulfed the field and came dangerously close to our house and barn. After the fire was put out, my parents felt our guilt and remorse and never mentioned it. We learned the mercy of compassion and forgiveness in addition to the foolishness of playing with matches in dry fields on windy days. My mother taught me honesty in a different way: When we stole balloons, she made us return them and individually admit our guilt, apologize, and offer to pay from our birthday money (we didn't get allowances). The humiliation of facing that storekeeper, whose sweet disposition and insistence that we keep the balloons, which made my guilt worse, has stayed with me until this day.

WEAKNESSES IN SUPPORT TECHNIQUES

The next two examples are letters of recommendation (also known as an appraisal letter), as frequently seen in the graduate school application process, and a job reference letter. A critique of both letters follows. In short, like so many academic and business documents, these letters could be made effective if more specific support was given in the form of examples, quotes, or anecdotes. In writing parlance, don't just mention the "what's," mention the "so what's." Mentioning the "so what's" provides support and indicates the reason why the writer is writing about something.

ACADEMIC LETTER OF RECOMMENDATION

Admissions Director:

It is my pleasure to serve as a reference for Richard Tyler in his application for admission to your graduate school. I have known Richard for fourteen years, first as an associate of his father (we worked together in a large U.S. conglomerate from 2000 to 2006). Later Richard worked for me at Xerox Corporation as an accountant and financial analyst.

Richard demonstrated a high level of intelligence, strong technical skills, and a very effective and positive way of interacting with people. He quickly gained the respect and support of his peers and seniors. He made a substantial contribution at Xerox Corporation during his period of service. I would particularly like to cite his originality and desire to innovate new systems and procedures.

Another remarkable quality worthy of mention is Richard's wide range of interests—from the specific and exacting profession of accounting and quantitative analysis to the broad interests that took him to Japan for study and international experience. This is a unique range.

Based on my 32-year career in the financial management of hi-tech companies and knowledge of many applicants and young graduates over the years, I would rank Richard in the top 10 percent of his peers now applying for admission.

Sincerely,
Frank B. Moore Jr.
VP Finance and Chief Financial Officer
Xerox Systems of America

JOB REFERENCE LETTER

To Whom It May Concern:

As a sales representative at the newly opened branch of Avon Cosmetic Products in Hong Kong, Judith was initially responsible for attending to the phones and walk-in customers. This was a new center for Avon International, and women's accessories was a brand new product area for the Hong Kong and PRC customers. Judith not only exceeded her sales quotas but also became our regional expert on how to adapt, modify, and package all our local products.

Besides having a very special organizational ability, Judith also has a wonderful way with her co-workers and customers. Co-workers listen to her advice and customers continue to buy from her. We have all watched Judith develop her marketing and sales skills. If she were not planning on leaving to go overseas, we would have offered her the position of director of our Beijing Avon Office, where she would not only administrate, but also train sales staff to open the China market.

As the person who started the Avon Hong Kong office and hired Judith, I am most proud of finding her for our company. She is extremely talented, diligent, and innovative, and all without formal business training. We sorely hate to lose her. I have never met another person who has greater potential to be a truly great marketer. Thus, I unqualifiedly and enthusiastically write this job reference letter. Your company will be proud of such an employee.

Sincerely,
Elizabeth Lee
Director, Avon Cosmetics (Hong Kong) Ltd.

CRITIQUE OF RECOMMENDATION LETTER

This recommendation letter follows a traditional format for a graduate school letter of recommendation. It cites at a minimum the context in which the recommender knows the candidate, and a quantifiable comparison is made of the candidate to others applying to graduate school. This letter constitutes a solid endorsement; the only criticism is that it misses a few opportunities to cite details in support of things said. For example, the reviewer is likely to respond to the recommender's statement "I would particularly like to cite his originality and desire to innovate new systems and procedures" by asking for details on these new systems and procedures. Moreover, the best professional recommendations may also make mention of a candidate's career aspirations, as well as areas of needed development. Sometimes the recommender cites anecdotes or quotes that other persons have made about the applicant as additional support.

CRITIQUE OF JOB REFERENCE LETTER

This job reference letter is a positive one, written in a light, colloquial tone. It comes across as warm and personable. A criticism of this letter lies in the lack of concrete details to support the recommender's statements. For example, the reviewer may want to know how much Judith exceeded her sales quota—by 1 percent or 200 percent—as well as the growth in sales of the Hong Kong office and how much of it should be credited to Judith's efforts. The recommender should give one example of how Judith adapted, modified, or packaged new products for the local market because the reviewer is no doubt interested. Perhaps the recommender could quote one of Judith's customers. Finally, the letter should mention one area where Judith is weak, to balance out the recommendation.

Principle 7

Personalize Your Examples

☞ **Principle #7: Add personal examples to make your writing more memorable.**

Principle 6—use specific and concrete words to support what you say—is arguably the most important of all writing techniques. Principles 6 and 7 work in tandem and are incredibly important tools in writing as well as in speech making. Often personal examples go hand in hand with the use of the personal pronoun "I." Do not be afraid to use this pronoun; it forces the writer to relate to the topic at hand in a way that is both personal and specific. Readers appreciate knowing how a situation relates to the writer (or speaker) in terms of his or her personal experience.

For example, the statement "Nigel is too busy to enjoy himself" is a general statement. The statement "Despite working at the local Co-op during the evenings, Nigel arrives home and diligently tackles his homework to prepare for next day's classes" is a personal statement that makes the same point.

Personalizing examples makes them more memorable. The following examples will give you some idea of how to use generic and detailed support points. Detailed support points give the reader an idea of what the writer personally came away with as a result of such and such experience.

NOTE ✍ In formal writing, as is the case when writing academic essays or business reports, it is standard practice to avoid the use of the personal pronoun "I." The likely reason for this is that the focus in formal writing is on the work (document) itself and not on the writer's personal opinions.

STATEMENT

I have analytical skills.

GENERIC SUPPORT POINT

Analytical skills help me work with numbers to both read and interpret financial statements. Analytical skills serve as objective measures and as the basis of good decision making.

DETAILED SUPPORT POINT

My time spent working at Accenture Consulting helped me develop an analytical mind set. I learned to reconcile what was said verbally with its financial reality. When a client said his or her problem was high costs, I systematically broke down total costs into their individual components. Once I knew where the numbers pointed, I looked for the stories behind these numbers. Sometimes the problem was not with high costs, as the client may have thought, but with another factor in the overall system.

STATEMENT

People are starving.

GENERIC SUPPORT POINT

People are starving—you can see it in their eyes and in the way their bones press against their skin.

DETAILED SUPPORT POINT

But it's the faces you can't forget; like images in a recurring nightmare, they keep coming back, haunted faces, staring blankly back from the windows of tumble-down hovels. The hollow lifeless eyes, skin stretched tight across backs, hands outstretched, dull listless eyes imploring. I move as if in a dream through the agony that is famine.

The above is an excerpt from the movie *The Year of Living Dangerously,* depicting the experiences of a young journalist stationed in Indonesia in the mid-1960s. This detailed support point also mimics the time-honored writer's adage "show, don't tell." Also, writing on an emotional level helps ensure that the reader gets a firsthand account, not a secondhand one.

Another potential weakness in support techniques occurs when students present records of extracurricular involvement when applying to college or graduate school. Because of the keen competition for entrance to highly rated schools, a candidate should present solid support for his or her involvement. Applicants often fall short, only mentioning the names of their extracurricular activities and the hours of involvement. Notice how much more meaningful a presentation becomes when a candidate not only provides proper support for what is being said but also personalizes the writing by providing detailed support points.

PRESENTATION OF A HIGH SCHOOL EXTRACURRICULAR ACTIVITY

Varsity Debate Team Member
Santa Rosa High School
Sept 2010 to May 2011

Time
Seven to ten hours per week excluding library research and occasional weekend travel

Description
Competed in high school NDT debate and participated in individual speaking events; won two regional debate tournaments, Pomona Invitational and West Coast Challenge.

Summary
Debate taught me four things:
- to organize and defend coherent arguments
- to speak under pressure
- to develop excellent research skills
- to formulate strategies for beating tournament competitors

My time spent in debate taught me to develop affirmative and negative briefs to support and defend the resolution at hand. I learned to be ever mindful of the importance of anticipating both sides of an argument. For every argument there is an equal and opposite argument. It is here that I gained my first real insights into an old tenet of philosophy: "Only through contrast do we have awareness."

Literary techniques also can be used to strengthen your personal or even business writing. Think of these writing techniques as optional tools to support the things you say in addition to examples and statistics.

ANECDOTES

Anecdotes are little stories used to embellish your point. For example, suppose you are writing about why we should follow our own path and not be unduly persuaded by the advice of others. You write:

This situation reminds me of the story of a young violinist who is burdened with thoughts of whether she possesses the talent to continue playing the violin and reach her lofty goal of becoming a virtuoso. Upon a fortuitous meeting with a master violinist, the young girl asks, "Will you listen to me play and tell me if you think I have the talent to be a virtuoso?" The master then responds, "If I listen to you play, and I feel you do not have the talent, what will you do?" The girl replies, "Since I value highly your opinion, I will stop playing." The master remarks, "If you would quit because of what I would say, then you obviously do not have what it takes to be a virtuoso."

QUOTATIONS

Including quotations, particularly those attributed to famous or well-known people, can be a persuasive tool. Quotations, when well chosen, make you look intelligent and/or add flair to your writing piece. Unfortunately, it is not always easy to recall an applicable quote from memory, and a little research will likely be needed. In addition to books that serve as quotation collections, there are many online quotation archives.

ANALOGIES

Analogies draw similarities between two otherwise dissimilar things and help the reader see a given relationship more clearly. For example, suppose you are writing an essay and want to stress the importance of making sales, particularly the relationship between the production department and the sales and marketing department. You might use the following "guns and bullets" analogy: "Production makes the bullets, marketing points the gun, and sales pulls the trigger." This makes clearer the idea that the production department is responsible for making products, while the marketing department is responsible for determining where sales are to be found, and the sales department is responsible for actually going out and making sales.

Say, for example, you wish to use an analogy to describe the difference between a person's personality and his or her mood swings. A climate-versus-weather analogy might be appropriate, such as: "Climate is like our fundamental personality traits, while weather is like our emotions and moods."

SIMILES AND METAPHORS

Similes compare two unlike things and are usually introduced by "like" or "as." An example of a simile is "A sharp mind is like a knife that cuts problems open." Similes are relatively easy to use and can be powerful tools in presenting your ideas.

Metaphors literally denote that one thing is another (instead of one thing being *like* another), and the words "as" or "like" are not used. An example of a metaphor is "He has nerves of steel."

Similes and metaphors are figurative comparisons, not actual comparisons. An example of an actual comparison is "Cindy is taller than Susan." Even though the focus of this book is on expository writing—and the use of analogies, similes, and metaphors present techniques which touch on creative writing—there are still uses for such literary techniques in everyday writing. Sales letters provide an everyday business example where the use of creativity is used to grab the reader's attention.

Ponder these opening lines:

A motivational or human resource company begins a sales letter with a simile:

Without a goal, a person is like a ship without a rudder.

A wine distributor advertises (by analogy):

Good wine and a good physician have one thing in common. They both can help extend your life!

A bungee jump operator employs a metaphor:

Do you have the heart of a lion?

<u>Exercise</u>

Try answering the following question:

How is a good idea like an iceberg?

Reflect on the statement above and write several one-sentence responses. Rest assured that by coming up with a half-dozen answers to this difficult example above, you will find crafting others for everyday writing purposes just that much easier. Possible answers are listed on page 120.

> Writing should be culled, but that's not the most important task: It's the second most important aspect of writing. The most important writing principle is that ideas should be sufficiently supported. It is detail that helps to make writing believable and memorable.

Principle 8

Keep It Simple

☞ **Principle #8: *Use simple words to express your ideas.***

The most fundamental way to simplify writing is to use simpler words. Simpler words—verbs, nouns, and adjectives—have broader meanings in English, while more complicated words have more specific meanings. Thus, you have a higher "margin of safety" when using simpler words.

Some writers adhere to the idea that "big words" are bad. The belief is that anyone who uses big words is just trying to impress the reader. The point embodied by Principle 8 is that the everyday writer should err on the side of using simpler words. That is not to say that there is no occasion for "bigger" or more specific vocabulary in writing, but rather that the writer should always consider how appropriate the vocabulary is for a given audience.

USING SIMPLER WORDS

The following chart shows how we may substitute a less familiar word with one that is more familiar and, therefore, easier to understand.

Acceded	☙ Agreed	Enumerate	☙ List
Accumulate	☙ Gather	Execute	☙ Carry out
Adaptability	☙ Adapt	Facilitate	☙ Make easy
Aggregate	☙ Total	Formulate	☙ Devise
Ameliorate	☙ Improve	Implementation	☙ Implement
Apprise	☙ Tell	Locality	☙ Place
Ascertain	☙ Find out	Materialize	☙ Develop
Attributable	☙ Due	Mitigate	☙ Lessen
Augment	☙ Increase	Modification	☙ Change
Cognizant	☙ Aware	Obfuscate	☙ Obscure
Demonstrate	☙ Show	Obviate	☙ Avoid
Diminutive	☙ Tiny	Proficiency	☙ Skill
Disseminate	☙ Send out	Resourcefulness	☙ Resourceful
Effectuate	☙ Carry out	Substantiate	☙ Prove
Endeavor	☙ Try	Utilize	☙ Use

NOTE ❧ Principle 6 addressed the use of specific, concrete words as opposed to general, vague ones. Principle 8 focuses on the use of simple words. The art of writing requires that the writer reconcile these two concepts. Small words are not necessarily specific words. For example, in the following two sentences—"It's a nice house" and "The overtime period was great"—the writer should consider replacing the words "nice" and "great" with more specific ones or, alternatively, opt for additional follow-up sentences. After all, the reader will likely wonder: what does "nice" or "great" really mean?

Exercise

Rewrite the following sentences by expressing the ideas more simply. The suggested answers are found on page 121.

1. There is considerable evidential support for the assertion that carrot juice is good for you.

2. We anticipate utilizing hundreds of reams of recycled copy paper in the foreseeable future.

3. This plan will provide for the elimination of inefficient shipping practices.

4. Educationwise, our schoolchildren should be given adequate training in the three Rs—reading, writing, and arithmetic.

5. Only meteorologists can perform a detailed analysis of changing climatic conditions.

6. With reference to the poem, I submit that the second and third stanzas connote a certain feeling of despair.

7. That dog is the epitome, the very quintessence, of canine excellence.

8. The hurricane destroyed almost all structures along the coastline. Most homes were destroyed when a confluence of water and wind joined forces to rip off roofs and collapse walls.

9. Which point of view do I adhere to? That's a good question. While I am against war, I also realize that some situations require the use of military force.

10. Like Napoleon's army that marched on Russia more than a century before, the German army was also unable to successfully invade Russia because its soldiers were inadequately prepared for winter conditions. German soldiers didn't even have proper winter clothing to withstand the subzero temperatures.

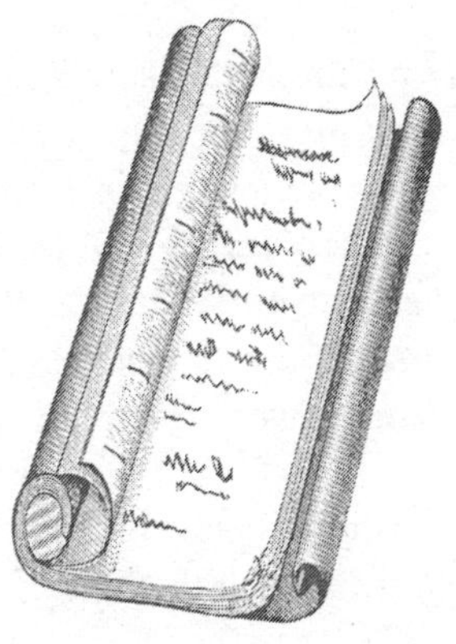

Principle 9

Cut Down Long Sentences

☞ **Principle #9: Make your writing clearer by dividing up long sentences.**

One way to make your writing clearer is to limit the use of long sentences. The easiest way to do this is to divide a long sentence into two or more shorter sentences. Caveat: The value of using short sentences does not mean that all sentences should be short. This would create a choppy style and is precisely where the art of writing needs to come into play. The writer must judge how to weave short sentences with longer ones, as well as how to use sentence variety (see Principle 14).

Here's an example of a very long sentence that needs help.

ORIGINAL

Leadership—whether on the battlefield or in another area, such as politics or business—can take place either by example or command, and Alexander the Great, renowned in both history and legend, is a good example of a military leader who led by both command and personal example, whereas Gandhi and Mother Teresa, both famous for their devotion to great causes, provide instances of people leading primarily by the inspiring power of personal example.

Cutting this large sentence into at least two or three smaller sentences would result in the following:

BETTER

Leadership can take place either by example or command. Alexander the Great is an example of a military leader who did both. Gandhi and Mother Teresa, on the other hand, led primarily by the inspiring power of personal example.

Here is another example of a "one-sentence" paragraph:

ORIGINAL

I entered the Neurological Faculty of the hospital and endured the next three months undergoing various diagnostic tests including EEG monitoring, in which my brain's electrical rhythms were monitored by electrodes placed on my scalp held by adhesive glue to record activity over a period of time, daily blood testing and blood counts, and all the required tests which subjected my brain to further diagnostic imaging from CAT scanning (computerized tomography), to an MRI (magnetic resonance imaging), to the costly PET scanning (positron emission tomography) and even the painful spinal fluid testing.

Obviously the previous sentence is running wild. Cut this large sentence into two or three smaller sentences as follows:

BETTER

I entered the Neurological Faculty of the hospital and endured three months of diagnostic tests including EEG monitoring, daily blood testing, and blood counts. EEG monitoring subjected my brain to electrical rhythms after electrodes were attached to my scalp. Other diagnostic tests further scrutinized my brain: CAT scans (computerized tomography), MRIs (magnetic resonance imaging), costly PET scans (positron emission tomography), and even painful spinal fluid testing.

There is power in short sentences, and their use should not be underestimated. Really short sentences (three to five words) catch the reader's eye and stand out as if naked. Their occasional use can add a dynamic touch to your writing. For example:

I like beer. Beer explains more about me than anything in the world. Who am I? I am the beer man—at least that is what many of my close friends call me.

One idea that carries merit is the "topic sentence, one-line rule." Topic sentences should ideally not be longer than one line to ensure that the reader grasps your point quickly.

In reference to beer and bare-naked sentences, the following sentences were used as part of a major campaign for dark beer:

Dark is different. Dark is exquisite. Dark is discerning. Dark is determined. Dark is mysterious. Dark is sensual. Dark is smooth. Dark is the other side of one's desire.

Principle 10

Eliminate Needless Words

☞ Principle #10: *Cut out redundancies, excessive qualification, and needless self-reference.*

Perhaps no one has ever captured (in 63 words!) the essence of brevity in writing as well as William Strunk, Jr.: "Vigorous writing is concise. A sentence should contain no unnecessary words, a paragraph no unnecessary sentences, for the same reason that a drawing should have no unnecessary lines and a machine no unnecessary parts. This requires not that a writer make all his sentences short, or that he avoid all detail and treat his subjects only in outline, but that every word tell."

REDUNDANCIES

Redundancy occurs when a writer needlessly repeats a word or an idea. It is redundant, for instance, to speak of an "inexperienced beginner." The word "beginner" by itself implies lack of experience. Redundant words or phrases can be eliminated without changing the meaning of the sentence.

Redundant	**Better**
advance notice	notice
any and all	any
ask the question	question
attractive in appearance	attractive
big in size	big
blue in color/blue colored	blue
charming in character	charming
combined together	combined
completely full	full
consensus of opinion	consensus
continues to remain	continues *or* remains
curious in nature	curious
descend down	descend
deliberately chosen	chosen
end result	result
exceptionally outstanding	exceptional
few in number	few
final outcome	outcome
hope and trust	hope *or* trust

if and when	if
lose out	lose
may perhaps	may *or* perhaps
modern world of today	modern world
mutual agreement	agreement
new initiatives	initiatives
new innovation	innovation
past experience	experience
past history	history
positive benefits	benefits
reiterate again	reiterate
reflect back	reflect
repeat (over) again	repeat
return back	return
sadly tragic	tragic
serious crisis	crisis
sink down	sink
tall in height	tall
true facts/hard facts	facts
undergraduate student	undergraduate
unexpected emergency	emergency
unique and one-of-a-kind	unique *or* one-of-a-kind
unsubstantiated rumors	rumors
until such a time	until
young juvenile	juvenile

EXCESSIVE QUALIFICATION

Occasional use of qualifiers will let the reader know that you are reasonable, but using such modifiers too often weakens your writing. Excessive qualification makes the writer sound hesitant, and adds bulk without adding substance.

Original *This rather serious leak may possibly shake the very foundations of the intelligence world.*

Better *This serious leak may shake the foundations of the intelligence world.*

And there is no need to quantify words that are already absolute.

ORIGINAL	BETTER
fairly excellent	*excellent*
truly unique	*unique*
the very worst	*the worst*
most favorite	*favorite*
quite outstanding	*outstanding*

Look also for opportunities to clean out qualifiers such as *a bit, a little, highly, just, kind of, most, mostly, pretty, quite, rather, really, slightly, so, still, somewhat, sort of.* Like *very, truly,* and *fairly,* they are all weakeners and are almost always unnecessary.

NEEDLESS SELF-REFERENCE

Avoid such unnecessary phrases as "I believe," "I feel," and "in my opinion." There is usually no need to remind your reader that what you are writing is your opinion.

EXERCISE 1

Rewrite the following sentences, cutting out redundancies. Suggested answers are found on page 122.

1. Attendees should be ready, willing, and able to adhere to the event's dress code and not wear casual clothes when formal attire is required.

2. A construction project that large in size needs an effective manager who can get things done.

3. The Acropolis Museum continues to remain a significant tourist attraction.

4. The ultimate conclusion is that physical and psychological symptoms are intertwined and difficult to separate.

5. The field superintendent's charisma and charming personality do not mask his scanty product or technical knowledge.

6. The recently observed trend of government borrowing may eventually create nations that are poorer and more impoverished than ever before.

7. These events—water shortages, chronic overcrowding, and rampant disease—have combined together to create a serious crisis.

8. Those who can find novel solutions to problems are few in number.

9. She has deliberately chosen to work for UNESCO.

10. Negotiation opens up many doors to peaceful settlement.

Exercise 2

Rewrite the following sentences, cutting out excessive qualification. Suggested answers appear on pages 122–123.

1. Peter is an exceptionally outstanding student.

2. You yourself are the very best person to decide what you should do with your life.

3. The propane tank is completely empty.

4. Joey seems to be sort of a slow reader.

5. There are very many reasons for the disparity in wealth among the world's nations.

6. Some experts believe that perhaps we are motivated simply by the desire to seek pleasure and to avoid pain.

7. In India, I found about the best food I have ever eaten.

8. She is a fairly excellent pianist.

9. The Hermitage Museum in St. Petersburg is filled with unique, one-of-a-kind paintings.

10. Needless to say, auditors should remain independent of the companies that they audit.

Exercise 3

Rewrite the following sentences, cutting out needless self-reference. Suggested answers are found on pages 123–124.

1. The speaker, in my personal opinion, is lost in details.

2. I feel, as many others do, that we ought to pay teachers as much as other professionals, such as doctors, lawyers, and engineers.

3. I do not think this argument can be generalized to those countries that have poor infrastructures.

4. My own experience shows me that wine is a fine social lubricant.

5. I'm really wondering whether more people would use the library if books and movies could be delivered to a person's home for a small fee.

6. Although I am no expert, I do not think that freedom of speech means that someone can scream "fire" in a crowded movie theatre and be held blameless.

7. If I had to venture a guess, I'd say that many individuals want to lose weight, but many fail simply because they do not decide on a diet program and then follow it diligently.

8. I must emphasize that I am not saying that the opposing argument is without merit.

9. If I were ever asked about the people that I find most inspiring, I would say that they are those individuals who are incredibly driven but incredibly humble.

10. It is my belief that to succeed in a relationship a person must be willing to give 70 percent and only expect to receive 30 percent.

Principle 11

Gain Active Power

☞ **Principle #11: Favor active sentences, not passive sentences.**

In general, favor the active voice over the passive voice because the active voice is more action-oriented. The active voice is both more direct and less verbose, cutting down on the number of needed words. For example, the sentence "Harry loved Sally" is written in the active voice and contains three words. The sentence "Sally was loved by Harry" is written in the passive voice and contains five words.

In a normal Subject-Verb-Object sentence, the doer of the action appears at the front of the sentence and the receiver of the action appears at the end of the sentence. Passive sentences are less direct because they reverse the normal Subject-Verb-Object sentence order, placing the doer of the action at the end of the sentence and the receiver of the action at the front of the sentence.

Passive *The company party was organized by the secretary.*

Active *The secretary organized the company party.*

Passive sentences may also fail to mention the doer of the action.

Passive *The writing of the report was easy.*

Active *She wrote the report easily.*

Writing students are so often told to avoid the passive voice that it is not hard to understand why the mere mention of the passive voice leads some zealots to blurt out "passive bad, active good." It is not categorically correct to say that we should always avoid the passive voice. Sometimes, the passive voice is effective or even necessary. Such is the case when the writer must decide whether to expose or hide the identity of the doer of the action.

EXAMPLE 1

Passive *Today, the computer files were erased.*
(The writer's goal is to hide the perpetrator.)

Active *Today, Calamity Jane erased the computer files.*
(The writer's goal is to expose the perpetrator.)

EXAMPLE 2

Another reason for using the passive voice is variety.

We sat through the visiting professor's intriguing lecture. The discussion centered on why people with higher I.Q.'s and lower E.Q.'s usually end up working for people with higher E.Q.'s but lower I.Q.'s. Afterwards, student questions were entertained.

The passive voice is appropriate when the performer of the action is unknown or unimportant. In the first example below, the extraction of oil is deemed important but the extractor is not. In the second example, the discovery of the pearl is important but the discoverer is either unknown or deemed unimportant.

EXAMPLES 3 & 4

Millions of barrels of oil were pumped from under the desert sand.

The world's largest pearl (6.4 kg) was discovered in the Philippines in 1934.

Finally, the passive voice is likely preferred when the receiver of the action is more important than the performer of the action.

EXAMPLE 5

Joyce Buckingham was awarded a medal by the committee organizers.

When imagining the passive voice, picture a young George Washington, hiding a hatchet behind his back, as he says to his father, "I cannot tell a lie: the cherry tree was chopped down."

Exercise

Rewrite the following sentences, replacing the passive voice with the active voice. Suggested answers are found on pages 124–125.

1. In premodern times, medical surgery was often performed by inexperienced and ill-equipped practitioners.

2. The main point made by the author can be found in the last paragraph.

3. Motivational courses are often attended by those who need them least, while they are not sought out by those who have greatest need.

4. The barbecue pits must be relocated where they can be used by campers.

5. Details of the peace agreement were ironed out minutes before the deadline.

6. Red Cross volunteers should be generously praised for their efforts.

7. Actor agreements will always be negotiated by an actor's agent before being signed by the actor.

8. Test results were posted with no concern for confidentiality.

9. The report was compiled by a number of clinical psychologists and marriage experts.

10. Without money, staff, and local government support, many diseases in less developed countries cannot be treated.

Principle 12

Favor Verbs, Not Nouns

☞ Principle #12: Avoid nominalizing your verbs and adjectives.

The word nominalization is a fancy sounding but important concept in writing. It describes the process by which verbs and adjectives are turned into nouns. Nominalizations weaken writing for a variety of reasons, mainly because they make sentences longer and force the reader to work harder to extract the sentence's meaning. The next page shows several examples of nominalizations.

Avoid turning verbs into nouns:

VERBS	NOUNS
reduce	*reduction*
develop	*development*
rely	*reliability*

So, "reduction of costs" is best written as "reduce costs," "development of a 5-year plan" is best written as "develop a 5-year plan," and "reliability of the data" is best written as "rely on the data."

Avoid turning adjectives into nouns:

ADJECTIVES	NOUNS
precise	*precision*
creative	*creativity*
reasonable	*reasonableness*

So, "precision of measurements" is best written as "precise measurements," "creativity of individuals" is best written as "creative individuals," and "reasonableness of working hours" is best written as "reasonable working hours."

Also, all verbs can be turned into nouns (called gerunds) when adding *-ing* (for example, speaking, carrying, and engaging).

EXAMPLE

Original *Is the drinking of alcohol by students allowed on campus?*

Better *May students drink alcohol on campus?*

The gerund "drinking" is best changed to the verb "drink."

Exercise

Rewrite the following sentences replacing nouns with either adjectives or verbs. Suggested answers are found on page 125.

1. Amateur cyclists must work on the development of their own training programs.

2. The inability to make decisions is a military leader's darkest enemy.

3. The expert panel's best estimate includes a 20 percent reduction in pollution as a result of the implementation of the new clean air bill.

4. Most dietitians advocate cutting down on the eating of fatty foods and reducing the intake of carbohydrates as the best means of losing weight.

5. Reasonableness and evenhandedness were not among the politician's strong suits.

6. The standardization of entrance exams helps ensure that students can apply to college and graduate school programs on an equal footing.

7. Hearing celebrities airing their political views on television should not be viewed as done in bad taste.

8. The applicability of using traditional accounting formulas for the valuation of Internet companies was never seriously questioned by investors prior to the first dot-com bust.

9. Our supervisor made a decision in favor of firing three employees.

10. Individuals who exhibit creativity and spontaneity should be encouraged to follow their dreams.

Principle 13

Use Parallel Forms

☞ Principle #13: **Express a series of items in consistent, parallel form.**

Parallelism in writing means that we should express similar parts of a sentence in a consistent way. Elements alike in function should be alike in construction. Parallelism builds clarity and power. Note the following sentence in parallel form: "The high school entrepreneur created, financed, and marketed the new miracle tool." Now compare this with a nonparallel form: "The high school entrepreneur was involved in the creation of a new miracle tool, secured financing for it, and spent time getting the product to market."

Consider the parallelism in the famous quote by former U.S. President John F. Kennedy:

Let every nation know, whether it wishes us well or ill, that we shall pay any price, bear any burden, meet any hardship, support any friend, oppose any foe to assure the survival and success of liberty.

Note how all the verbs are in parallel form. Also, ponder the parallelism of this famous spiritual verse.

Blessed are the poor in spirit: for theirs is the kingdom of heaven. Blessed are they that mourn: for they shall be comforted. Blessed are the meek: for they shall inherit the earth. Blessed are they which do hunger and thirst after righteousness: for they shall be filled.

Parallelism may involve any part of speech, but especially verbs, prepositions, and conjunctions. They may also involve the articles *a, an,* and *the.*

Parallelism must be observed closely when we list a series of items. The rule here is that either we repeat the word before every element in a series or include it only before the first item. Anything else violates the rules of parallelism governing a series of items. Your treatment of the second element of the series determines the form of all subsequent elements.

EXAMPLE 1

Original *Miguel went to Chile, Peru, and to Ecuador.*

Correct *Miguel went <u>to</u> Chile, <u>to</u> Peru, and <u>to</u> Ecuador.*

Correct *Miguel went <u>to</u> Chile, Peru, and Ecuador.*

EXAMPLE 2

Original *She likes sun, sand, and going to the sea.*

Correct *She likes the sun, the sand, and the sea.*

Correct *She likes the sun, sand, and sea.*

EXAMPLE 3

Original *The prime minister had met with military personnel, listened to his closest advisors, and had studied a recent poll result before deciding on military action.*

Correct *The prime minister had met with military personnel, had listened to his closest advisors, and had studied a recent poll result before deciding on military action.*

Correct *The prime minister had met with military personnel, listened to his closest advisors, and studied a recent poll result before deciding on military action.*

EXERCISE 1

Rewrite the following sentences using parallel structure. Suggested answers appear on page 126.

1. Despite winning the lottery, the elderly couple said they planned to spend money only on a new tractor, new stove, and a new porch.

2. Olympic volunteers were ready, fully able, and were quite determined to do a great job.

3. The documentary was interesting and replete with pertinent information.

4. Wayne Gretsky was well-liked by his teammates and National Hockey League fans respected him.

5. Students can log onto Facebook, spend time reading email messages, review some blog posts, and then tweet with joy.

6. The fund manager based his theory on stock performance, bond performance, and on other leading economic indicators.

7. The dancer taught her understudy how to move, to dress, how to work with choreographers and deal with photographers.

8. Just as the sound advice of a good lawyer can help win a court case so too can a sports match be won by the sound advice of a good coach.

9. According to the Buddhist mantra, fearfulness, feelings of anger, and needless desire lead to suffering. Eliminate fearfulness, feelings of anger, and needless desire and you eliminate suffering.

10. My objections regarding the pending impeachment are, first, the personal nature of the matter; second, that it is partisan.

ELLIPTICAL EXPRESSIONS

Parallelism also involves rules for when we can acceptably eliminate words in a sentence and still retain clear meaning. Three potentially tricky situations may arise when using verbs, prepositions, and correlative conjunctions. In the case of verbs (or verb forms) and prepositions, it is okay to omit a second verb or preposition if it is the same as the first. To check for faulty parallelism, complete each component idea in a sentence and make sure each part of the sentence can stand alone. For instance, in the sentence "The speech was informative and funny," there is no need to say "The speech was informative and was funny," since the second verb "was" is the same as the first, and need not be written out.

Verbs

Original *In my favorite Japanese restaurant, the sushi is excellent and the drinks expensive.*

Correct *In my favorite Japanese restaurant, the sushi is excellent and the drinks are expensive.*

Definition ☙ The verb in the second part of the sentence is different from the verb used in the first part of the sentence and must be written out.

Prepositions

Original *John is interested but not very good at golf.*

Correct *John is interested in but not very good at golf.*

Definition ☙ The preposition in the second part of the sentence is different from the preposition used in the first part of the sentence and must be written out.

Correlative Conjunctions

Correlative conjunctions include "either ... or," "neither ... nor," "not only ... but also," and "both ... and." If a verb is placed before the first component part in the correlative construction, then the verb need not be repeated. If the verb is placed after the first component part in the correlative construction, then it must be placed after the second item as well.

Original *She not only likes beach volleyball but also snow skiing.*

Correct *She likes not only beach volleyball but also snow skiing.*

Correct *She not only likes beach volleyball but also likes snow skiing.*

NOTE ✍ The first correct version above is arguably more popular.

Exercise 2

Rewrite the following sentences using parallel structure. Suggested answers are found on pages 127–128.

1. The painting may be done either with watercolors or oils.

2. Tasmania has and always will be an island.

3. Who is not interested and astounded by this fact?—A million seconds ago was 11.5 days ago; a billion seconds ago was 31 years ago; a trillion seconds ago was 310 centuries ago or 31 millennia ago!

4. Massage creates a relaxing, therapeutic, and rejuvenating experience both for your body and your well-being.

5. Samantha is intrigued but not very proficient at handwriting analysis.

6. A good scientist not only thinks logically but also creatively.

7. Brian will not ask nor listen to any advice.

8. Either we forget our plans or accept their proposal.

9. A dilemma facing many young professionals is whether to choose to work for money or to work for enjoyment.

10. Neither should one lie to good friends nor be so patronizing as to not tell them the truth.

> Writing is part science and part art. That writing be structured and conform to rules is science. That writing may vary with each situation is art.

Principle 14

Capitalize on Sentence Variety

☞ Principle #14: Vary the length and beginnings of your sentences.

The normal sentence pattern in English is subject-verb-object (S-V-O), as seen in the example "I play tennis." Most sentences should follow this subject-verb-object sequence because it produces the most power. However, if all sentences follow this order, our writing becomes choppy and monotonous. Particularly noticeable are series of sentences all beginning the same way, especially with "I" or "we." Here are ten ways to vary sentence beginnings.

WITH A SUBJECT

Customers can tell us why products sell if we take the time to listen to them.

Definition ☙ The subject is what or whom the sentence is about.

WITH A PHRASE

For this reason, no product is to be built until we know a market exists for it.

Definition ☙ A phrase is a group of words that does not contain a verb.

WITH A CLAUSE

Because human beings are complex, the sales process cannot be reduced to a simple formula.

Definition ☙ A clause is a group of words that does contain a verb.

WITH AN ARTICLE

A good batting average is an arguably more important statistic in baseball than is the number of home runs achieved.

Definition ☙ There are three articles in English—*a, an,* and *the.*

WITH A VERB

Try not to text during the speech.

Definition ☙ A verb is a word that expresses an action or a state of being.

WITH AN ADVERB

Understandably, students like to hear entrepreneurs speak of rags-to-riches stories.

Definition ☙ An adverb is a word that modifies a verb, an adjective, or another adverb. When adverbs are used to begin sentences (usually followed by a comma), they can be referred to as "opening sentence" adverbs.

WITH ADJECTIVES

Intelligent and compassionate, Dorothy has the ingredients to be a leader.

Definition ☙ An adjective is a word used to modify or describe a noun or pronoun.

WITH A GERUND

Traveling to a country is more meaningful when you first invest time reading about its geography and history.

Definition ☙ A gerund is a noun formed with *-ing*. Informally it is said to be "a noun that looks like a verb."

WITH AN INFINITIVE

To be a monk, a person must be able to relinquish selfishness in order to concentrate on a higher goal.

Definition ☙ An infinitive is a noun that is formed by a verb preceded by *to*.

WITH CORRELATIVE CONJUNCTIONS

Not only poverty but also pollution threatens the development of the third world.

Definition ☙ A conjunction is a word that joins or connects words, phrases, clauses, or sentences. A correlative conjunction joins parts of a sentence that are of equal weight. Four common correlative conjunctions include "either ... or," "neither ... nor," "not only ... but (also)," and "both ... and."

EXERCISE

Selling is difficult. It requires practical experience and personal initiative.

To practice this principle, rearrange the above sentence to satisfy the different headings below. You may have to change the content of the sentence for the purpose of this exercise. Suggested answers appear on pages 128–129.

1. With a Subject
2. With a Phrase
3. With a Clause
4. With an Article
5. With a Verb
6. With an Adverb
7. With Adjectives
8. With a Gerund
9. With an Infinitive
10. With Correlative Conjunctions

Principle 15

Choose an Appropriate Tone

☞ **Principle #15: Write with a positive, personal tone.**

Tone is a difficult thing to describe; some define it as the writer's attitude. Tone occurs along two major dimensions: positive or negative and formal or informal. Today, a positive and personal tone is appropriate on most writing occasions. One way to control writing tone is through your choice of positive versus negative words. Use positive words whenever possible; readers instinctively dislike being told what is not true as opposed to what is true. Thus, even negative forms can be turned into positive expressions.

POSITIVE VS. NEGATIVE TONE

Negative *The store will close at 7 p.m.*

NOTE ☙ This uses a negative verb "close."

Positive *The store will remain open until 7 p.m.*

NOTE ☙ This uses a positive adjective "open."

Negative *The plan is not sound.*

NOTE ☙ This uses a negative word; it tells us what isn't true as opposed to what is true.

Positive *The plan has drawbacks.*

NOTE ☙ This states deficiencies in a positive manner; it tells us what is true.

FORMAL VS. INFORMAL TONE

Writing may have a formal or an informal tone. Two factors that influence formality are the use of contractions and personal pronouns.

Use of Personal Pronouns

Add personal pronouns to make your writing more informal and personable.

No pronouns *Please send any follow-up questions to the customer service department.*

Pronouns *If you have any follow-up questions, please contact our customer service department.*

No pronouns	*The Chief Executive Officer is aware that strengthening product quality is the key to turning around the company.*
Pronouns	*Our Chief Executive Officer believes that we need to strengthen product quality in order to turn the company around.*

A complete list of personal pronouns include:

1st person	*I, me, my, mine, we, us, ours*
2nd person	*you, your, yours*
3rd person	*he, she, they, him, her, them, it, his, hers, its, their, theirs*
Also	*who, whom, whose*

Use of Contractions

Add contractions (for example, *can't, isn't, shouldn't, won't*) if you want your writing to come across as informal.

No contractions	*The stockholders have not voted on a new Chief Executive Officer.*
Contractions	*The stockholders haven't voted on a new Chief Executive Officer.*

Other factors also affect whether a document is considered formal, informal, or semi-formal (see following page). A personal letter or e-mail is typically informal, while a business report is formal. A business letter is a good example of a semi-formal document: It usually contains informal characteristics (for example, use of contractions, first-person pronouns, colloquial expressions, and simple or non-technical vocabulary) as well as formal characteristics (for example, formal salutations and signatures).

CHARTING THE FORMAL AND INFORMAL TONES

The two "pyramids" below highlight the characteristics of a formal and informal tone.

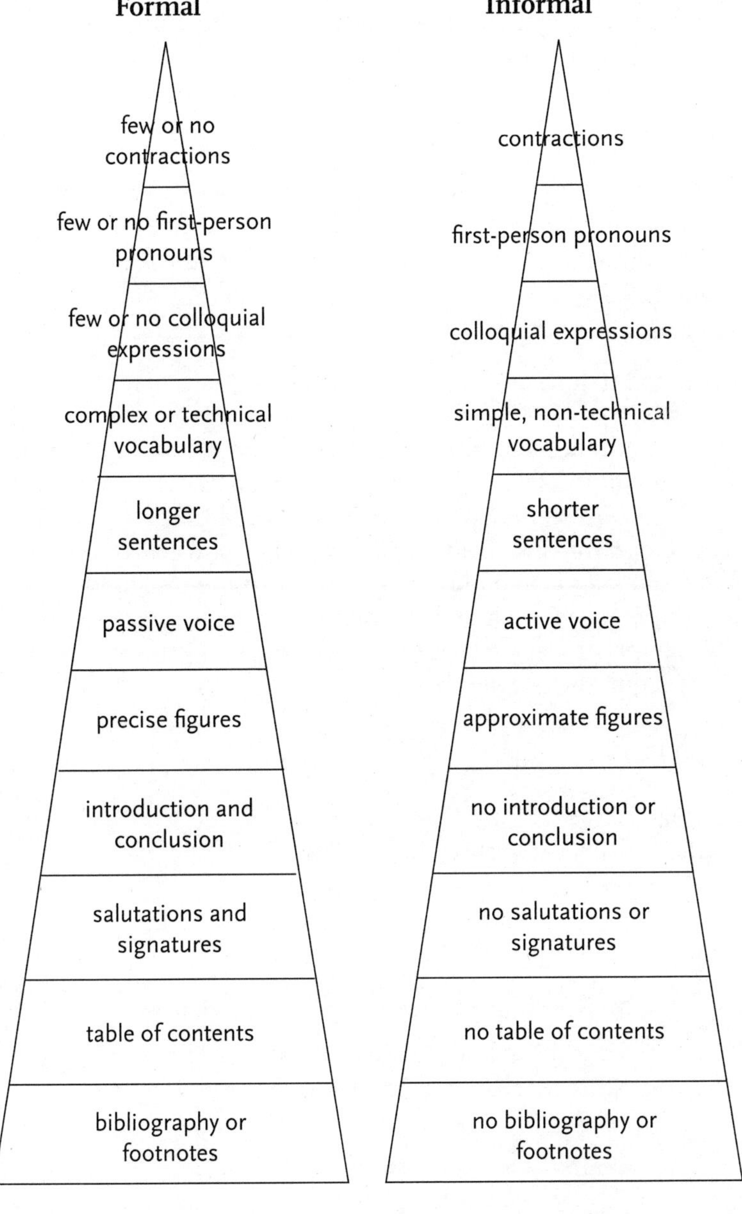

NOTE ↜ Although the use contractions is now widespread, there are two theories on the effect of their use. The first theory or majority view is to use contractions because they reinforce a personal tone. The second or minority view is that although contractions are fine for use in writing e-mails and personal letters, it is preferable to avoid them in formal documents such as essays and reports.

EXERCISE

Make this letter "warmer" by using a more positive and personal tone. This is a semi-formal document, and it is recommended that contractions not be used. A suggested revision is found on page 129.

Dear Mr. Jones:

Comptronics Inc. deeply regrets the problems experienced with your notebook computer, Model 580G. The company's engineers examined the unit and decided that the problems were so massive that they were not able to make repairs. The two remaining options are either to take a refund on the unit, or to request replacement with a new model. Please inform the service department of a decision, and Comptronics Inc. will quickly respond.

Sincerely,

Mr. Do Good
Service Representative
Comptronics Inc.

Tone is attitude. A formal tone is like formal attire that keeps distance between the writer and reader. Most writing favors an informal tone.

Principle 16

Keep Your Writing Gender Neutral

☞ **Principle #16: Avoid using the masculine generic to refer to both genders.**

The masculine generic refers to the sole use of the pronoun "he" or "him" when referring to situations involving both genders. Avoid using "he" when referring to either a he or a she; likewise, avoid using "him" when referring to either a him or a her. Be sensitive in acknowledging both sexes. Because 50 percent of any general readership is likely female, it is not only politically astute but fair-minded to avoid using the masculine generic.

Consider the following sentences from a female perspective.

ORIGINAL

Today's chief executive must be extremely well rounded. He must be not only corporate and civic minded but also environmentally focused and entrepreneurially spirited.

There are essentially two ways to remedy this. Replace "he" with "he or she," or recast the sentence in the plural, using "they" or "them."

BETTER

Today's chief executive must be extremely well rounded. He or she must be not only corporate and civic minded but also environmentally focused and entrepreneurially spirited.

EQUALLY PROPER

Today's chief executives must be extremely well rounded. They must be not only corporate and civic minded but also environmentally focused and entrepreneurially spirited.

A final way to address the problem, especially when writing longer documents, is to alternate between the use of "he" and "she." The disadvantage in this approach, however, is that the arbitrary, alternate use of these two pronouns may annoy the reader and cause confusion.

We must also watch for and replace words that represent the masculine generic. Here is a partial list:

MASCULINE GENERIC	BETTER
ad man	*advertising executive*
anchorman	*anchor*
chairman	*chair, chairperson*
Englishmen	*the English*
fireman	*firefighter*
man-hours	*work-hours, person-hours*
mankind	*humans, humankind, humanity*
policeman	*police officer*
postman, mailman	*mail carrier, postal agent*
salesman	*salesperson, sales representative*
self-made man	*self-made person*
businessman	*businessperson*
congressman	*member of Congress, Senator, Representative*
spokesman	*spokesperson*
landlord	*land owner*
layman	*layperson*
man-made	*synthetic, artificial*
workman	*worker*

It is sometimes necessary to replace the feminine generic:

FEMININE GENERIC	BETTER
housewife	*homemaker*
maid/cleaning lady	*domestic, housekeeper*
maiden name	*birth name, former name*
secretary (office)	*office assistant*
stewardess	*flight attendant*

Part III

Readability

Put it before them briefly so they will read it, clearly so they will appreciate it, picturesquely so they will remember it and, above all, accurately, so they will be guided by its light.

—Joseph Pulitzer

Principle 17

Capitalize on Layout and Design

☞ **Principle #17: Add more space around your writing to increase readability.**

The easiest way to make writing more readable is to increase your document's margin. Also, ensuring that a blank line separates paragraphs will let your composition breathe. Avoid writing one big block of words pressed tight against the edges of the page. Two versions of an identical document appear on the next two pages; the second is easier to read simply because it employs more space in the margins and between paragraphs.

ORIGINAL VERSION

Paradox of Our Time by Dr. Bob Moorehead

The paradox of our time in history is that we have taller buildings but shorter tempers, wider freeways, but narrower viewpoints. We spend more, but have less; we buy more, but enjoy less. We have bigger houses and smaller families, more conveniences, but less time. We have more degrees but less sense, more knowledge, but less judgment, more experts, yet more problems, more medicine, but less wellness.

We drink too much, smoke too much, spend too recklessly, laugh too little, drive too fast, get angry too quickly, stay up too late, get up too tired, read too little, watch TV too much, and pray too seldom.

We have multiplied our possessions, but reduced our values. We talk too much, love too seldom, and hate too often.

We've learned how to make a living, but not a life. We've added years to life, not life to years. We've been all the way to the moon and back, but have trouble crossing the street to meet a new neighbor. We conquered outer space, but not inner space. We've done larger things, but not better things.

We've cleaned up the air, but polluted the soul. We've conquered the atom, but not our prejudice. We write more, but learn less. We plan more, but accomplish less. We've learned to rush, but not to wait. We build more computers to hold more information, to produce more copies than ever, but we communicate less and less.

These are times of fast foods and slow digestion, of tall men and short character, of steep profits and shallow relationships. These are the days of two incomes but more divorce, of fancier houses, but broken homes. These are days of quick trips, disposable diapers, throwaway morality, overweight bodies, and pills that do everything from cheer, to quiet, to kill. It is a time when there is much in the showroom window and nothing in the stockroom.

IMPROVED VERSION

Paradox of Our Time by Dr. Bob Moorehead

The paradox of our time in history is that we have taller buildings but shorter tempers, wider freeways, but narrower viewpoints. We spend more, but have less; we buy more, but enjoy less. We have bigger houses and smaller families, more conveniences, but less time. We have more degrees but less sense, more knowledge, but less judgment, more experts, yet more problems, more medicine, but less wellness.

We drink too much, smoke too much, spend too recklessly, laugh too little, drive too fast, get angry too quickly, stay up too late, get up too tired, read too little, watch TV too much, and pray too seldom.

We have multiplied our possessions, but reduced our values. We talk too much, love too seldom, and hate too often.

We've learned how to make a living, but not a life. We've added years to life, not life to years. We've been all the way to the moon and back, but have trouble crossing the street to meet a new neighbor. We conquered outer space, but not inner space. We've done larger things, but not better things.

We've cleaned up the air, but polluted the soul. We've conquered the atom, but not our prejudice. We write more, but learn less. We plan more, but accomplish less. We've learned to rush, but not to wait. We build more computers to hold more information, to produce more copies than ever, but we communicate less and less.

These are times of fast foods and slow digestion, of tall men and short character, of steep profits and shallow relationships. These are the days of two incomes but more divorce, of fancier houses, but broken homes. These are days of quick trips, disposable diapers, throwaway morality, overweight bodies, and pills that do everything from cheer, to quiet, to kill. It is a time when there is much in the showroom window and nothing in the stockroom.

Principle 18

Employ Readability Tools

☞ Principle #18: Make key words and phrases stand out.

Painters, sculptors, musicians, professional photographers, and poets are but a few individuals highly adept at judging what effect stylistic additions and deductions will have on an overall composition. Writing is also a balancing act. The writer seeks to retain those greater elements that most define a writing piece while looking for smaller adornments to bolster its appearance and readability. In the writing arena, such adornments might include boldface type, italics, dashes, bullets, enumerations, and shading.

BOLDS

Bolds (boldface type) may be used to emphasize keywords and help key ideas "jump out" at the reader. Bolds are especially useful for flyers, résumés, and other documents in which the reader may spend only a brief time reviewing. Italics or underlining can do the same job as bold type, though care must be exercised not to overdo it. For example, rarely do we want to see bolds and italics used in the same paragraph. One unwritten rule of writing and editing is to never use bolds, italics, and underlines together (ditto for bolds, italics, and full caps in combination). Be aware that if you use boldface type too liberally, you will dull the effect and perhaps patronize the reader.

ITALICS

There is artistry in the occasional use of italics. Italics, like bolds, serve similar purposes. Consider using italics to highlight certain key words, especially those that show contrast, or for small words, especially negative words such as *not, no,* and *but.* Be careful of overusing italics because they are tiring on the eye and can make the page look busy.

For stylistic purposes, many examples in this book appear in italics in order to distinguish them from explanatory text. Note that such text would not normally be italicized.

DASHES

Dashes can be used to vary the rhythm of a sentence and to place emphasis on words and phrases in a more dynamic manner than could be achieved through the use of a comma (or pair of commas) or semicolon.

The world's oldest dated book—the Diamond Sutra—is an elaborately decorated book containing a beautiful cover piece. Written in 868 A.D., it was discovered in 1907 in a cave near Dunhuang, China.

Note how the dashes in the previous example make the reference to the book appear more dramatic than in the example below, which contains commas:

The world's oldest dated book, the Diamond Sutra, is an elaborately decorated book containing a beautiful cover piece. Written in 868 A.D., it was discovered in 1907 in a cave near Dunhuang, China.

BULLETS

Bullets (•) are effective tools for paraphrasing information, especially for presenting information in short phrases when formal sentences are not required. Bullets are most commonly used when preparing résumés, slides, or flyers. Bullets are not, however, recommended for use in the main body of an essay or report unless they are included within a table. It is also not considered good practice in formal writing to use hyphens (-) or asterisks (*) in place of bullets.

ENUMERATIONS

Enumerations involve the numbering of points. Listing items by number is more formal but very useful for ordering ideas or data.

EXAMPLE 1

I feel that my greatest long-term contributions working in this field will be measured by (1) my ability to find ways to define and quantify, in dollars and cents, the benefits of ethics and corporate citizenship, and (2) my ability to sell corporations on the proactive benefits of these programs as a means to market their company, products, and employees.

EXAMPLE 2

Each letter in the word "s.u.c.c.e.s.s." embodies a single action:

1. *Super effort*
2. *Unusual drive*
3. *Copy what works.*
4. *Change what doesn't.*
5. *Exercise now and cut out excess.*
6. *Save a little more, spend a little less.*
7. *Start all over again the very next day.*

SHADING

Shading creates contrast on the page and can be a great device for formatting business reports. For example, you can highlight the start of each section of a report by using shaded section headings. Within the pages of a report, shading is often used to tint the top row (header row) of a table. Flyers also commonly use shading to call out information.

RÉSUMÉ EXAMPLE

The following is an excerpt from a résumé. Résumés provide a classic example of the use of readability tools, particularly in terms of bullets, bolds, and italics.

PROFESSIONAL EXPERIENCE

2012–present **BANK OF AMERICA,** Hartford, Conn.

Financial Analyst

- Analyzed branch performance and devised new strategies to improve regional market share. Formulated a two-year marketing plan for two branches.
- Developed a new commission system and assisted in its implementation.
- Presented tax saving strategies and advice on investment portfolio compositions for principal clients.

Principle 19

Use Headings and Headlines

☞ Principle #19: **Use headings and headlines to divide or summarize your writing.**

Because organization is particularly important in academic writing, which tends to be longer, and because time and money are of critical importance in business, both headings and headlines help convey information efficiently. Headlines are similar to headings; the difference lies in their length and purpose. Headings are usually a couple of words in length; headlines are usually a line or two in length. The purpose of headings is to divide information under sections; the primary purpose of headlines is to summarize or paraphrase information that follows.

EFFECTIVE USE OF HEADINGS

With the use of headings in the document below, the writer is able to direct the reader's attention; without headings, the reader would have a harder job of accessing the information efficiently.

The Four Cs

Color
The most desirable diamonds are colorless. The color scale starts at D and descends through Z. Although the best color is D (colorless), diamonds also come in a range of natural fancy tones, such as blue, pink, green, and red. Believe it or not, these fancy diamonds are particularly rare, and like their colorless counterparts, can also fetch a high price tag.

Clarity
Gemologists refer to imperfections in diamond clarity as "inclusions"; the fewer inclusions, the more valuable the stone.

Cut
What makes a diamond stand out beyond any other precious gemstone? Certainly the way it sparkles. While nature determines the color and clarity of a stone, diamond cut is solely dependent upon the skill of the cutter.

Carat Weight
The word carat comes from the carob seeds that were used to balance scales in ancient times. Carat therefore refers to size. It is not necessarily true that the larger the carat, the more valuable the diamond. The value of a stone will always be a combination of the four Cs: color, clarity, cut, and carat size.

EFFECTIVE USE OF HEADLINES

Headlines are effective tools in summarizing complete sections of a business report or personal essay. The headlines below appear in italics.

The Land, Sea, and Sky Must Guide Me

The land, the sky, and the sea: These three environments and the experiences they have given me have influenced and helped shape who I am today.

When I go back to the land in the northern part of Denmark, I walk across the fields and hear the birds singing.

The land has taught me to appreciate my base and family stability. ____
____
___________________________.

The smallest corals in bright colors can be poisonous, while the sharks may be friendly.

When scuba diving, I have learned to expect the unexpected.
____
____
____.

The sky is a reminder that many things are possible even though they seem beyond our reach.

Sky diving has encouraged me to stretch and reach new heights. ____
____
_______________.

One of the big challenges I am meeting in life is the challenge of being successful in both my personal and career life. In meeting these challenges, all of my influences must guide me – the land, the sea, and the sky.

Principle 20

Go Back and Rework Your Writing

☞ *Principle #20: Wait until your writing stands still before you call it finished.*

Rare is the writer who can sit down and knock out a perfect writing draft without corrections. Most proficient writers take at least three drafts to finish short pieces of writing. For example, you may be writing a cover letter to accompany your updated résumé. First, you write to get your ideas down on paper. Second, you edit through what you have written, add detail, make connections, and make corrections. Third, you wait twenty-four hours and reread, making minor changes. The longer the work, the more times this process is repeated for individual sections.

The number of drafts required for an entire work depends on the work's length and complexity. A two-line office memo is likely to be done in a single draft because it is short and simple. A one-page poem might take more than a dozen drafts because it is longer and more difficult.

WHEN IS IT REALLY FINISHED?

Making changes to your writing is annoying and grueling. But eventually, with changes made, you will likely be satisfied with what you have written and not want to add or delete anything. This is the point at which your writing is finished—your writing is "standing still." Unpolished writing is like shifting sand in a desert storm. Eventually the storm ceases, and the sand sits still. The word "finished," when referring to writing, should really be enclosed in quotation marks because writing is never actually finished. With respect to writing done for everyday purposes, completion is an end in itself. However, for more permanent written works, such as novels, writing can be continued indefinitely because it can always be improved. Even published books can be reworked and reedited. Weeks, months, and years after a book is published, an author will invariably contemplate changes.

APPRECIATE THE PROCESS

Writing is a creative process. You discover things as you force yourself to write. What is especially satisfying is turning "junk" writing into something worthwhile. When you put together a lengthy piece, such as a personal essay or business report, you will naturally begin by writing some areas well. Other areas you'll not be satisfied with, and those must be reworked.

Let's call the parts you like "flowers" and the parts you dislike "dirt." As you focus your efforts on the "dirt," you begin to make improvements, and sometimes to your surprise, these areas become as good as, or better than, one or more of the "flowers." This is extremely satisfying. You are inspired. You gain energy.

You now try to improve other "dirt" areas until there are none left. Later, you go back to an original "flowered" area and make it even better, thus raising it up one notch from anything done before. The writing process is a ongoing process of producing flowers and dirt.

Most people hate reworking their writing. It is human nature. The pressure and agony of writing is one reason why alcohol has been humorously dubbed "the occupational hazard of professional writers." It is not writing per se, but the rewriting and redrafting process that can drive a person to drink. Worse is the reality of knowing that even before you begin to write—no matter how well you write—your writing will require revision. Fortunately, for most students and business professionals, the everyday writing process is not filled with the same emotional highs and lows as it is for a person who makes a living from writing.

It is a great feeling to look at something you wrote a long time ago, be it an old college essay, business report, personal letter, or poem, and say to yourself, "Wow, this is funny. Some of this stuff blows me away! How did I come up with it?" There is no absolute answer. Skill, luck, boldness, and naiveté are key ingredients in the writing process.

Appendixes

The pleasure of the first draft lies in deceiving yourself that it is quite close to the real thing. The pleasure of the subsequent drafts lies partly in realizing that you haven't been gulled by the first draft.

—Julian Barnes

Appendix 1. Summary of the 20 Writing Principles

Part I: Structure

Principle 1	Write your conclusion and place it first.
Principle 2	Break your subject into two to four major parts and use a lead sentence.
Principle 3	Use transition words to signal the flow of your writing.
Principle 4	Use the six basic writing structures to put ideas in their proper order.
Principle 5	Finish discussing one topic before going on to discuss other topics.

Part II: Style

Principle 6	Use specific and concrete words to support what you say.
Principle 7	Add personal examples to make your writing more memorable.
Principle 8	Use simple words to express your ideas.
Principle 9	Make your writing clearer by dividing up long sentences.
Principle 10	Cut out redundancies, excessive qualification, and needless self-reference.
Principle 11	Favor active sentences, not passive sentences.
Principle 12	Avoid nominalizing your verbs and adjectives.

Principle 13	Express a series of items in consistent, parallel form.
Principle 14	Vary the length and beginnings of your sentences.
Principle 15	Write with a positive, personal tone.
Principle 16	Avoid using the masculine generic to refer to both genders.

Part III: Readability

Principle 17	Add more space around your writing to increase readability.
Principle 18	Make key words and phrases stand out.
Principle 19	Use headings and headlines to divide or summarize your writing.
Principle 20	Wait until your writing stands still before you call it finished.

PRINCIPLE 3 (Page 27)

The most probable solution to the whale essay is to organize the sentences in the following order: 5, 2, 1, 4, 3.

THE WHALE

The whale is the largest mammal in the animal kingdom. When most people think of whales, they think of sluggish, obese animals, frolicking freely in the ocean and eating tons of food to sustain themselves. When people think of ants, on the other hand, they tend to think of hardworking underfed creatures transporting objects twice their body size to and from hidden hideaways. However, if we analyze food consumption based on body size, we find that ants eat their full body weight every day, while a whale eats the equivalent of only one-thousandth of its body weight each day. In fact, when we compare the proportionate food consumption of all living creatures, we find that the whale is one the most food-efficient creatures on earth.

NOTE ☙ In the above paragraph, the conclusion appears in the last line. If a writing piece is very short and uncomplicated, there is little harm in putting the conclusion at the end. This may seem like an exception to Principle 1, and it is, but it represents the art of writing as opposed to the science of writing.

PRINCIPLE 6 (Page 45)

1. Joannie has a German Shepherd and a Siamese cat.

2. The vacation cost nearly $5,000.

3. Rainbows contain a full spectrum of colors, including red, orange, yellow, green, blue, indigo, and violet.

4. Sheila is 5'10" tall and has an attractive, baby-shaped face.

5. Many economists think that the Federal Reserve Bank's failure to lower bank interest rates is the reason for the current economic downturn.

6. Firms should use billboard advertising because it is low-cost and can increase sales as much as 10 percent in a given region.

7. Tim often misplaces his car keys.

8. The contestant was eliminated in the first round because she couldn't remember that Antarctica is one of the seven continents.

9. Fresh produce, small cans, and large boxes line each row of the grocery store from floor to ceiling.

10. Mr. and Mrs. Jones spend most of their time together, often laughing at each other's jokes.

PRINCIPLE 7 (Page 59)

- A good idea is cool!
- A good idea stands out.
- A good idea may get a chilly reception.
- A good idea can easily disappear.
- A good idea sure seems natural.
- A good idea has a big effect on its surroundings.
- You have to go a long way to find a good idea.
- A good idea takes time to form.
- If you overlook a good idea, it can sink you.
- You only see part of a good idea because there is more to it than meets the eye.
- There is a lot of depth in a good idea, but not everyone appreciates it.
- One-tenth of the benefit of a good idea is clearly visible, but nine-tenths of the long-term benefits lie below the surface.

PRINCIPLE 8 (Page 62)

1. Recent studies suggest that carrot juice is good for you.

2. We expect to use hundreds of reams of recycled copy paper in the next 12 months.

3. This plan will eliminate inefficient shipping practices.

4. Our schoolchildren's education should emphasize the three Rs—reading, writing, and arithmetic.

5. Only meteorologists can analyze changing climatic conditions.

6. When the poet wrote the second and third stanzas, he must have felt despair. (Or: I feel despair when reading the poem's second and third stanzas.)

7. That is a fine dog.

   Note that a follow-up sentence is likely required to supply more details as to what a fine dog is.

8. The hurricane destroyed almost all structures along the coastline.

9. While I am against war, I also realize that some situations require the use of military force.

10. Like Napoleon's army that marched on Russia more than a century before, the German army was also unable to successfully invade Russia because its soldiers were inadequately prepared for winter conditions.

NOTE ☙ The last three examples above require cutting out sentences to achieve simplicity. Such sentences may repeat information that the reader has otherwise gleaned from sentences that come immediately before or after.

PRINCIPLE 10, EXERCISE 1 (Page 70)

1. Attendees should adhere to the event's formal dress code.

2. A construction project that large needs an effective manager.

3. The Acropolis Museum remains a significant tourist attraction.

4. The conclusion is that physical and psychological symptoms are intertwined.

5. The field superintendent's charisma does not mask his poor technical knowledge.

6. The recent trend of government borrowing may create poorer nations.

7. These events—water shortages, chronic overcrowding, and rampant disease—have combined to create a crisis.

8. Few people can find novel solutions to problems.

9. She has chosen to work for UNESCO.

10. Negotiation opens many doors to peaceful settlement.

PRINCIPLE 10, EXERCISE 2 (Page 71)

1. Peter is an exceptional student.

2. You are the best person to decide what you should do with your life.

3. The propane tank is empty.

4. Joey is a slow reader.

5. There are many reasons for the disparity of wealth among the world's nations.

6. Some experts believe that we are motivated simply by the desire to seek pleasure and to avoid pain.

7. In India, I found the best food I have ever eaten.

8. She is an excellent pianist.

9. The Hermitage Museum in St. Petersburg is filled with unique paintings.

10. Auditors should remain independent of the companies that they audit.

PRINCIPLE 10, EXERCISE 3 (Page 72)

1. The speaker is lost in details.

2. We ought to pay teachers as much as other professionals, such as doctors, lawyers, and engineers.

3. This argument cannot be generalized to those countries with poor infrastructures.

4. Wine is a fine social lubricant.

5. Would more people use the library if books and movies could be delivered to a person's home for a small charge?

6. Freedom of speech does not mean that someone can scream "fire" in a crowded movie theatre and be held blameless.

7. Many individuals want to lose weight, but many fail simply because they do not decide on a diet plan and then follow it diligently.

8. I am not saying that the opposing argument is without merit. (Or: The argument has merit.)

9. The most inspiring individuals are those who are incredibly driven but incredibly humble.

10. To succeed in a relationship, a person must be willing to give 70 percent and only expect to receive 30 percent.

PRINCIPLE 11 (Page 76)

1. In premodern times, inexperienced and ill-equipped practitioners often performed medical surgery.

2. The author makes the main point in the last paragraph.

3. Those who attend motivational courses often need them least, while those who choose not to attend usually need them most.

4. We must relocate the barbecue pits so campers can use them.

5. Negotiators ironed out the details of the peace agreement minutes before the deadline.

6. Citizens should generously praise Red Cross volunteers for their efforts.

7. A talent agent always negotiates an actor's agreement before an actor signs it.

8. The institute posted test results with no concern for confidentiality.

9. A number of clinical psychologists and marriage experts compiled the report.

10. Without money, staff, and local government support, doctors cannot treat diseases in less developed countries.

NOTE ~ In examples 5, 8, and 10 above, the suggested solutions involve supplying a subject (that is, *negotiators, institute, and doctors).*

PRINCIPLE 12 (Page 79)

1. Amateur cyclists must develop their own training programs.
2. A military leader who is unable to decide faces a dark enemy.
3. The expert panel estimates that the new clean air bill, when fully implemented, will reduce pollution by 20 percent.
4. According to most dietitians, the best way for dieters to achieve weight loss is to reduce their intakes of fatty foods and carbohydrates.
5. The politician was neither reasonable nor evenhanded.
6. Standardized entrance exams help ensure that students can apply to college and graduate school programs on an equal footing.
7. Celebrities should feel free to air their political views on television.
8. Prior to the first dot-com bust, investors never seriously questioned whether traditional accounting formulas should be used to value Internet companies.
9. Our supervisor decided to fire three employees.
10. Creative, spontaneous individuals should be encouraged to follow their dreams.

PRINCIPLE 13, EXERCISE 1 (Pages 82–83)

1. Despite winning the lottery, the elderly couple said they planned to spend money only on a new tractor, a new stove, and a new porch.

2. Olympic volunteers were ready, able, and determined to do a great job.

3. The documentary was interesting and informative.

4. Wayne Gretsky was well-liked by his teammates and respected by National Hockey League fans.

   If the subject, Wayne Gretsky, is understood, we could write: His teammates liked him and National Hockey League fans respected him.

5. Students can check Facebook, read email messages, review blog posts, and then joyfully send tweets.

6. The fund manager based his theory on stock performance, on bond performance, and on other leading economic indicators.

7. The dancer taught her understudy how to move, dress, work with choreographers, and deal with photographers.

8. Just as the sound advice of a good lawyer can help win a court case, so too can the sound advice of a good coach help win a sports match.

9. According to the Buddhist mantra, fear, anger, and desire lead to suffering. Eliminate fear, anger, and desire and you eliminate suffering.

10. My objections regarding the pending impeachment are, first, the personal nature of the matter; second, the partisan nature of the matter.

PRINCIPLE 13, EXERCISE 2 (Page 85)

1. The painting may be done either with watercolors or with oils.

   Or: The painting may be done with either watercolors or oils.

2. Tasmania has been and always will be an island.

3. Who is not interested in and astounded by this fact?—A million seconds ago was 11.5 days ago; a billion seconds ago was 31 years ago; and a trillion seconds ago was 310 centuries ago or 31 millennia ago!

4. Massage creates a relaxing, therapeutic, and rejuvenating experience both for your body and for your well-being.

   Or: Massage creates a relaxing, therapeutic, and rejuvenating experience for both your body and your well-being.

5. Samantha is intrigued with but not very proficient at handwriting analysis.

6. A good scientist not only thinks logically but also thinks creatively.

   Or: A good scientist thinks not only logically but also creatively.

7. Brian will not ask for or listen to any advice.

8. We either forget our plans or accept their proposal.

   Or: Either we forget our plans or we accept their proposal.

9. A dilemma facing many young professionals is whether to work for money or to work for enjoyment.

10. One should neither lie to good friends nor be so patronizing as to not tell them the truth.

    Or: Neither should one lie to good friends nor should one be so patronizing as to not tell them the truth.

PRINCIPLE 14 (Page 89)

1. With a subject: Selling is difficult because it requires practical experience and personal initiative.

2. With a phrase: For many reasons, selling is difficult.

3. With a clause: Because it requires both practical experience and personal initiative, selling is difficult.

4. With an article: The reason selling is difficult is that it requires both practical experience and personal initiative.

5. With a verb: Use your experience and your instincts and you will succeed in a selling career.

6. With an adverb: Traditionally, the terms "sales" and "marketing" were used interchangeably.

7. With adjectives: Confident and resourceful, a salesperson must possess these two key traits.

8. With a gerund: Requiring a person to have both practical experience and personal initiative, selling is difficult.

9. With an infinitive: To be an effective salesperson, one must be able to accept disappointment and work in an unpredictable environment.

10. With correlative conjunctions: Not only practical experience but also personal initiative is required to be a good salesperson.

PRINCIPLE 15 (Page 94)

When making the letter more positive, eliminate negative words such as "not able" and "so massive." Also add personal pronouns such as "you" and "yours." Moreover, "our company" sounds better than "Comptronics"; "our service department" sounds better than "the service department." The original letter contains two personal pronouns, namely *your* and *they*; the letter below contains ten uses of personal pronouns, namely *our, your, you, our, you, you, us, your, our,* and *your.*

Dear Mr. Jones:

Our company deeply regrets hearing of the problems you experienced with your notebook computer, Model 580G. Our engineers have examined the unit and believe that the best solution involves one of two choices:

(1) You receive a full refund on the unit, or (2) you allow us to replace your computer with a new model.

Please let our service department know your decision.

Sincerely,

Mr. Do Good
Service Representative
Comptronics Inc.

Where there is an open mind
there will always be a frontier.

—Charles F. Kettering

Selected Bibliography

The Chicago Manual of Style. 15th ed. Chicago: University of Chicago Press, 2003.

Clark, Roy Peter. *Writing Tools: 50 Essential Strategies for Every Writer.* New York: Little, Brown and Company, 2008.

Ehrenhaft, George. *Barron's SAT Writing Workbook*. 2nd ed, Barron's Educational Series. Hauppage, NY: Barron's, 2009.

Encarta Webster's Dictionary of the English Language. 2nd ed. New York: Bloomsbury, 2004.

Fogiel, Max. *The English Handbook of Grammar, Style, and Composition*. Piscataway, NJ: Research and Education Association, 1987.

King, Stephen. *On Writing: A Memoir of the Craft*. New York: Pocket Books, 2000.

Kramer, Melinda, Glenn H. Leggett, and C. David Mead. *Prentice Hall Handbook for Writers*. 11th ed. Englewood Cliffs, NJ: Prentice Hall, 1995.

Merriam Webster's Collegiate Dictionary. 11th ed. Springfield, MA: Merriam Webster, 2005.

Oxford Dictionary of English. 2nd ed. New York: Oxford University Press, 2005.

Ritter, Robert M. *The Oxford Style Manual*. New York: Oxford University Press, 2003.

Strunk, William, Jr., and E. B. White. *The Elements of Style*. 4th ed. New York: Allyn and Bacon, 2000.

Warriner, John E. *English Composition and Grammar: Complete Course*. Orlando, FL: Harcourt Brace Jovanovich, 1988.

Wikipedia, The Free Encyclopedia, s.v. "Writing Style," http://en.wikipedia.org/wiki/Writing_style.

Wilbers, Stephen. *Keys to Great Writing*. Cincinnati, OH: Writer's Digest Books, 2000. Reprinted in paperback, 2007.

Williams, Joseph M. *Style: Toward Clarity and Grace*. Chicago: University of Chicago Press, 1995.

Winokur, Jon. *Advice to Writers: A Compendium of Quotes, Anecdotes, and Writerly Wisdom from a Dazzling Array of Literary Lights*. New York: Vintage, 2000.

Zinsser, William. *On Writing Well: 30th Anniversary Edition: The Classic Guide to Writing Nonfiction*. New York: Harper Paperbacks, 2006.

Index

About the Author

Brandon Royal is an award-winning writer whose educational authorship includes *Power Grammar, Power Thinking,* and *Power Math.* During his tenure working in Hong Kong for US-based Kaplan Educational Centers—a Washington Post subsidiary and the largest test-preparation organization in the world—Brandon honed his theories of teaching and education and developed a set of key learning "principles" to help define the basics of writing, grammar, math, and reasoning.

A Canadian by birth and graduate of the University of Chicago's Booth School of Business, his interest in writing began after completing writing courses at Harvard University. Since then he has authored a dozen books and reviews of his books have appeared in *Time Asia* magazine, *Publishers Weekly, Library Journal of America, Midwest Book Review, The Asian Review of Books, Choice Reviews Online, Asia Times Online,* and About.com.

Brandon is a five-time winner of the International Book Awards, a six-time gold medalist at the President's Book Awards, as well as recipient of the 2011 "Educational Book of the Year" award as presented by the Book Publishers Association of Alberta. He has also been a winner or finalist at the Ben Franklin Book Awards, the Global eBook Awards, the IPPY Awards, the USA Book News "Best Book Awards," and the *Foreword* magazine Book of the Year Awards.

To contact the author:
E-mail: contact@brandonroyal.com
Web site: www.brandonroyal.com

JAICO PUBLISHING HOUSE

Elevate Your Life. Transform Your World.

ESTABLISHED IN 1946, Jaico Publishing House is home to world-transforming authors such as Sri Sri Paramahansa Yogananda, Osho, The Dalai Lama, Sri Sri Ravi Shankar, Sadhguru, Robin Sharma, Deepak Chopra, Jack Canfield, Eknath Easwaran, Devdutt Pattanaik, Khushwant Singh, John Maxwell, Brian Tracy and Stephen Hawking.

Our late founder Mr. Jaman Shah first established Jaico as a book distribution company. Sensing that independence was around the corner, he aptly named his company Jaico ('Jai' means victory in Hindi). In order to service the significant demand for affordable books in a developing nation, Mr. Shah initiated Jaico's own publications. Jaico was India's first publisher of paperback books in the English language.

While self-help, religion and philosophy, mind/body/spirit, and business titles form the cornerstone of our non-fiction list, we publish an exciting range of travel, current affairs, biography, and popular science books as well. Our renewed focus on popular fiction is evident in our new titles by a host of fresh young talent from India and abroad. Jaico's recently established Translations Division translates selected English content into nine regional languages.

In addition to being a publisher and distributor of its own titles, Jaico is a major national distributor of books of leading international and Indian publishers. With its headquarters in Mumbai, Jaico has branches and sales offices in Ahmedabad, Bangalore, Bhopal, Chennai, Delhi, Hyderabad, Kolkata and Lucknow.

SINCE 1946